LGBTQAI+ Books for Children and Teens

Providing
a Window
for All

LGBTQAI+
BOOKS
*for Children
and Teens*

Foreword by
JAMIE CAMPBELL NAIDOO

**Christina Dorr
and Liz Deskins**

ALA
Editions

CHICAGO | 2018

© 2018 by the American Library Association

Extensive effort has gone into ensuring the reliability of the information in this book; however, the publisher makes no warranty, express or implied, with respect to the material contained herein.

ISBNs
978-0-8389-1649-0 (paper)
978-0-8389-1693-3 (PDF)
978-0-8389-1692-6 (ePub)
978-0-8389-1694-0 (Kindle)

Library of Congress Cataloging in Publication Control Number: 2017052430

Cover design by Krista Joy Johnson. Book design by Alejandra Diaz in the Questa, Noyh A Bistro and Azo Sans typefaces.

⊚ This paper meets the requirements of ANSI/NISO Z39.48–1992 (Permanence of Paper).

Printed in the United States of America
22 21 20 19 18   5 4 3 2 1

To the founding students of our GSA at WMS
for the powerful group we began together.
And for my nephew, Robb,
who showed me how to be myself
when the rest of the world thinks you should be someone else.

— CHRISTINA —

To Bob and Brett: I was fortunate to grow up in a home
where color and race were unimportant; everyone was welcome.
But it was not until I had a gay child that I truly understood
that love is love is love.

— LIZ —

Contents

LGBTQAI+ Books Save Lives

JAMIE CAMPBELL NAIDOO, PHD

Quality books representing culturally diverse children and their families can serve as mirrors, reflecting one's culture; windows, providing glimpses into the lives of other cultures; or doors, allowing one to walk in someone else's shoes.[1] A good book can also save lives and build bridges between seemingly disparate worlds.

As a gay child raised in rural Kentucky, I was surrounded by classmates, religious leaders, and caring adults who clearly conveyed that something was wrong with me because I did not fit in to society's strict views of gender expression and masculinity. When I was younger, I played with dolls and pink ponies, cooked mud pies and held tea parties, and dressed in my grandmother's scarves and costume jewelry. In kindergarten, I was Raggedy Ann in the Halloween parade and often found myself in the "play house" learning center where I could cook and play "daddy" to all the babies. In first grade, my prized possession was a pair of rainbow roller skates. Most of my friends were girls. When I grew older, though, I was discouraged from playing with girls and participating in "girl" activities. In junior high, it became horrifying clear that I was different from other boys. While my male classmates were interested in sports and the physical development of my female friends, I was more interested in crafts and the physique of guys in gym class. Initially, I would tell myself that I was scientifically studying the other boys to compare physical changes in our bodies, while also wishing that I could look like them. Eventually, I admitted to myself that I found some of them attractive. But I knew better than to tell anyone! There was only one student in our small school who was out, and everyone heard the slurs hurled toward him and saw the blind eyes of teachers as he was being bullied.

Like many queer teens in rural areas or hostile environments, I learned how to live firmly in the closet. I was alone and thought there was no one like me. Books with LGBTQAI+ (lesbian, gay, bisexual, transgender, queer/questioning, asexual, intersex, and other diverse identities and expressions) characters were not plentiful and certainly not present in my conservative school library. The public library in our town, run by volunteers from the Women's Club, was open only two days a week. Even if the library had stocked copies of the few gay-friendly young adult books available in the late 1980s and early 1990s, I would not have checked them out due to the lack of privacy inherent in a paper-based library card system that allowed anyone to track borrowers of a particular title. It wasn't until I was in college that I found a book that truly served as the mirror for which I had long been searching. Todd Brown's *Entries from a Hot Pink Notebook* was my savior. I could completely relate to the main character's experiences; the fourteen-year-old protagonist could have been me in high school. I used the book to help sort out some of my feelings related to religion, sexuality, and identity; and eventually I used it to come out to my mother.

While this book has a special place in my heart, thinking about it also brings up resentment. Where were books like this when I needed them as a child? As a teenager? Why did I have to wait until college before I could see myself in the pages of a book? Rainbow families, or families with LGBTQAI+ children, teens, caregivers, and/or family members, are everywhere, found in every community and present in schools and libraries across the country. Like all children, children in rainbow families deserve to see their experiences and family structures represented in the books they read and in library activities. Yet many youth today are still robbed of these opportunities because librarians are afraid to have LGBTQAI+ books in their collections. Some library workers find the books' topics deplorable, while others are afraid of censorship challenges. According to the American Library Association's Office of Intellectual Freedom, almost all of the challenged books for children and teens have diverse content and many represent LGBTQAI+ experiences.[2]

I often wonder how contemporary youth in rainbow families feel when all the library displays, programs, and collections feature cisgender, heterosexual characters and families with a mother and a father. Do they possess enough self-awareness to be angry, or will that come only later as they mature into young adulthood? Do they feel as alone and self-loathing as I did because I thought something was wrong with me?

Contrary to what some educators, librarians, and caregivers may erroneously believe, children's and young adult books with LGBTQAI+ characters and families are often no more about sex than are books with heterosexual characters and families. Often, those opposing the use of LGBTQAI+ literature with youth take the "sex education" perspective, suggesting that these books are used to indoctrinate readers into condoning and engaging in certain types of sexual behaviors. To demonstrate the absurdity of this belief, let's consider the children's picture book *Donovan's Big Day* by Lesléa Newman. This charming book captures the joys of a young boy, Donovan, as he prepares to serve as the ring bearer in his two mothers' wedding. When young readers encounter this book, they are introduced to a peer who is excited about his caregivers' union. They are not learning about lesbian sexual practices. The same holds true when children read *Lilly's Big Day* by Kevin Henkes. This book captures the varied emotions that mouse Lilly experiences as she serves as honorary flower girl in her teacher Mr. Slinger's wedding. Although Mr. Slinger is straight, readers are not learning about heterosexual bedroom practices when they read this book. Yet many educators will hesitate to use Newman's book while widely embracing Henkes's work.

LGBTQAI+ children's books and young adult books are critical to help children see those metaphorical mirrors and windows in literature. As Dorr and Deskins succinctly point out in this volume, these books can be used in many different activities in classrooms and libraries to spark critical conversations and foster understanding of "the other" in society. The authors have selected a variety of popular and noteworthy titles for children, tweens, and teens with LGBTQAI+ content. Their programming recommendations and links to author websites and book discussion guides will prove useful to librarians, educators, and other caring adults interested in creating welcoming spaces for rainbow families. While readers may not find every noteworthy LGBTQAI+ youth title listed, the suggestions for the highlighted books can be used to jumpstart program planning for other titles that represent LGBTQAI+ experiences.

Recently, I was talking with a friend about her nephew, whom she suspects is gay. Unfortunately, the child's father is homophobic and vehemently discourages the boy from expressing his identity. Does this child have access to library collections with books that show him he's okay even if his father says he's worthless? Are his teachers and librarians astute enough to help him find the right book at the right time to help him survive his homophobic family? Or will he end up a statistic, crumpling under societal pressures to conform to such a degree that he takes his own life?

Books can save lives. I found *Entries from a Hot Pink Notebook* during a dark time in my life. This right book at the right time changed everything for me. Fortunately, many affirming, LGBTQAI+ children's and young adult books exist today that can equally save lives if librarians and educators will only add them to their collections. Professional books such as this one are crucial to identifying and using materials that build bridges of understanding and create safe spaces where all are welcome. Are you up to the challenge of saving lives over avoiding potential negative feedback? With this volume in your hands, the answer can be a resounding "Yes!"

NOTES

1. Rudine Sims Bishop, "Selecting Literature for a Multicultural Curriculum," in *Using Multiethnic Literature in the K–8 Classroom*, ed. Violet Harris (Norwood, MA: Christopher-Gordon Publishers, 1997), 1–20.
2. James LaRue, "Defining Diversity," Banned and Challenged Books, American Library Association, Office for Intellectual Freedom, accessed June 7 2017, www.ala.org/bbooks/diversity; Nick Duffy, "LGBT Books Dominate 2016's Most-Banned List," *Pink News*, September 27, 2016, www.pinknews.co.uk /2016/09/27/lgbt-books-dominate-2016s-most-banned-list.

BIBLIOGRAPHY

Brown, Todd. *Entries from a Hot Pink Notebook*. New York: Washington Square Press, 1995.

Henkes, Kevin. *Lilly's Big Day*. New York: Greenwillow Books, 2006.

Newman, Lesléa. *Donovan's Big Day*. Illustrated by Mike Dutton. Berkeley, CA: Tricycle Press, 2011.

Windows into Reality

Many people likely remember where they were and how they felt on June 26, 2015, when the Supreme Court of the United States, in a tight and emotional vote, ruled to legalize same-sex marriage. We were attending the American Library Association Annual Conference in a most appropriate setting, San Francisco. The joyful heartbeat of that decision was palpable, as cries of celebration rang throughout the conference and the entire city. This landmark decision forced the country to turn a corner in regard to attitudes, legal rights, and the freedom to discuss LGBTQAI+ (lesbian, gay, bisexual, transgender, queer, asexual, intersex, and other terms that describe members of the community) concerns like no other phenomenon before ever had.

And, as expected, the response to that decision caused a backlash by ultraconservative groups. For example, the Religious Freedom Restoration Act passed in Indiana and elsewhere effectively twists the 1993 federal law of the same name by providing "ways that could allow businesses a wider berth to discriminate"[1] against the legal rights of the LGBTQAI+ community by claiming that the provision of service would infringe upon the business owner's religious freedoms. The transgender bathroom law passed in North Carolina, and in other states, is a "wide-ranging bill barring transgender people from bathrooms and locker rooms that do not match the gender on their birth certificates."[2] It effectively creates a discrimination policy, forcing transgender individuals into possible predatory situations. And the June 2016 massacre of more than fifty people at a gay Latino bar in Orlando might be the most insidious recent event in the United States.

These issues have caused deep emotional reactions on both sides. The country takes three steps forward, only to take two steps back. And consensus won't be reached for many years, if ever, but nonetheless, a corner has been turned. The time has come for librarians, teachers, and other professionals who work with children and young adults to open discussion, encourage understanding, and hopefully garner acceptance. And the avenue we use to advocate is through high-quality literature for all.

Why share LGBTQAI+ literature with all children? Because, we argue, it's an issue of basic human rights—rights that all of us deserve. We no longer hesitate to share books about other forms of diversity: race, ethnicity, socioeconomic status, age, language, women's issues, and more. Why are we still hesitant to share books about sexual orientation, gender identity and expression, and nontraditional family structures with all children?

Here's how a good friend of Christina's, an excellent, forward-thinking, literature- and discussion-loving fifth grade teacher, describes his worries:

> [Sharing these books] is a prickly topic. It's like walking through thorns, and you don't want to get pricked. You plan out where you want to walk, so you don't get pricked. . . . I'm self-conscious about the topics. . . . The developmental level of my students must lead me how to share. . . . I worry about parents' anger.

After some discussion, Christina realized that he was essentially worried about the sexual issues of the literature. He said, "I wouldn't share any books or discussion about heterosexual relationships, and I won't with homosexual relationships, either." This led to a great discussion that included, "Of course you wouldn't discuss either. But that's not what sharing LGBTQAI+ books is all about. It's about fairness, equality, and understanding, dealing with basic human rights for all," and also to the acknowledgment that that's where his class discussions should focus. We parted as good of friends as ever, with more for both of us to ponder.

Liz asserts, as a parent of a gay son, which was evident when he was a child, that she was always searching in books for role models and examples of positive gay people and experiences to share with him. In the 1980s, there were very few picture books available, and it was not until her son was in high school when they found good books that had characters with which he could identify. Liz's favorite book, published in 1987, but not available in the United States until 1997, was *The Straight Line Wonder* by Mem Fox. Liz's son was headed for a career as a ballet dancer, and seeing this line who moved the way that made it happy instead of staying a straight line like its friends, gave her encouragement that her son would be happy if he followed his dream. While it is not quite that easy in real life, this book became a symbol for them.

Arguments for inclusion of these books in libraries and curricula for all children come from a wide variety of sources. In a powerful talk at the 2016 Virginia Hamilton Conference (VHC), poet Nikki Grimes asserted that "hatred is not inevitable . . . [because] the most important common denominator is the human heart . . . ; [therefore,] what's missing in the talk about diversity in literature is that they're needed for everyone."[3] At the same conference, author Margarita Engle, concurred, stating, "When we read about others' lives, we learn about empathy, the first step in peacemaking."[4]

At the 2016 *School Library Journal* (*SLJ*) Day of Dialog, author Jason Reynolds argued for inclusion of diverse books, because "the authenticity you find in another person is the authenticity you find in yourself. . . . [R]eaders [may not know] the actions in the book, but can recognize the truths . . . and that truth lies not in disseminating the facts but our ability to disseminate the questions."[5] What a powerful argument for inclusion, discussion, and finding the common ground of our human experiences!

Gene Luen Yang, author of the Printz Award–winning young adult graphic novel *American Born Chinese* and the fifth National Ambassador for Young People's Literature named by the Library of Congress, had this to say at a conference we recently attended: "Books themselves are ambassadors . . . books can be advocates. . . . This is why we need diverse books [as they] teach kids to love others [and act as a] moral foundation."[6]

Following a random link on a website we'd never perused before, we discovered a freelance writer who had this to say:

> No matter who you are—black, white, gay, straight, male, female—reading provides you with an opportunity to see inside someone else's life. Books are the perfect tools to help you navigate through the diverse experiences of other people, and they have the ability to help you better understand and empathize with someone outside of your own circumstances.[7]

Rudine Sims Bishop, an enduring voice in the field of diverse children's literature, writes:

> When children cannot find themselves reflected in the books they read, or when the images they see are distorted, negative, or laughable,

they learn a powerful lesson about how they are devalued in the society of which they are a part. . . .

Children from dominant social groups have always found their mirrors in books, but they, too, have suffered from the lack of avail-ability of books about others. They need the books as windows onto reality, not just on imaginary worlds. They need books that will help them understand the multicultural nature of the world they live in, and their place as a member of just one group, as well as their con-nections to all other humans.[8]

And maybe most simply and directly put by author Kelly Barnhill, "If you change the narrative you change the world."[9] So let's all take the prickly path and begin to change the world by first looking briefly back at the roots of children's and young adult (YA) LGBTQAI+ literature, and then at the world today, and then forward into what we can create.

HISTORY OF CHILDREN'S AND YOUNG ADULT LGBTQAI+ LITERATURE

There is not a long history of gay literature for children and young adults. The first book considered by some to be a book for children in the LGBTQAI+ spectrum was published in 1936. *The Story of Ferdinand*, written by Munro Leaf, was the first book that portrayed a gender-nonconforming character, although not one who was openly gay. Ferdinand was a bull that would rather sniff flowers than behave like an aggressive typical bull. The story was very popular, and Walt Disney even made it into an award-winning animated film in 1938.

In 1969, the first YA book to deal with LGBTQAI+ content was written, John Donovan's *I'll Get There. It Better Be Worth the Trip.*, published by Harper and Row. In it, thirteen-year-old Davy loses the grandmother he lived with and is sent to live with his divorced and unhappy mother, where he feels like all he has left is his dog. He meets and connects with a class-mate and they form a relationship, which progresses until Davy's mother finds them in bed with their arms around each other. She puts an end to the relationship temporarily, but by the end of the story, they seem to have reconciled, and one is led to believe there will be a happy ending. Interest-ingly, this book was published at the beginning of the Stonewall Rebellion.

By the 1970s, a few children's picture books dealing with LGBTQAI+ issues had been published in foreign countries. One example is *Jenny Lives with Eric and Martin* by Susanne Bösche, published in Denmark in 1981 and translated into English in 1983. This black-and-white photographically illustrated picture book presented everyday activities Jenny did with her father and his boyfriend. Jenny's mother lived down the street and was also portrayed positively. The author's intent was to allow children to see a variety of families and family life. Many called it "homosexual propaganda," and it met with great challenge and censure.[10] The first picture book of record that dealt openly with a lesbian couple was *When Megan Went Away* by Jane Severance and Tea Schook. Published in 1979 by a small feminist press, it was not widely circulated, which was unfortunate because it was a realistic portrayal of a lesbian relationship and the difficulties inherent in such a relationship during that time period.

Arizona Kid by Ron Koertge, published in 1989 by HarperCollins, was a critical book at the time for several reasons:

- It was published at the beginning of the Stonewall Rebellion.
- It openly talked about AIDS.
- It shared healthy gay relationships.

Weetzie Bat by Francesca Lia Block, published by HarperCollins, was another groundbreaker. Often called an urban fantasy set in altered Los Angeles, Weetzie, and her best gay friend, Dirk, live their own lives full of acceptance and joy. When a genie gives Weetzie three wishes, she asks for a love for Dirk named Duck, one for her named My Secret-Agent Lover Man, and a house where they can all live. These things manifest, and though the magic is almost incidental, these wish fulfillments and the life they create make this story an impactful one. Although it contains references to gay love, rape, raising children out of wedlock, AIDS, and death, because these are just inferred or mentioned and the characters carry on and decide to live happily, if not happily ever after, it became a touchstone novel for many young people for the next decade. Of course, the very mention of those topics led to its being challenged and censored in many school and public libraries.

Probably for many today, the most widely recognized LGBTQAI+ book for children is *Heather Has Two Mommies*, and this was one of the first titles to go mainstream. Lesléa Newman, the author, felt that all children needed to see themselves and their families reflected in books. This idea is an important example of windows in children's and YA books, that is, the value of seeing one's face, culture, community, and family reflected in what one reads. Because, as Bishop asserts, "when there are enough books available that can act as both mirrors and windows for all our children, they will see that we can celebrate both our differences and our similarities, because together they are what make us all human."[11] Newman explains her reasoning for writing the book:

> When I was growing up, there were no picture books that showed a Jewish family like mine. I remember wishing that there were. So when someone asked me to write a book about a little girl with two moms for her daughter to read, I was happy to do so. I wrote *Heather Has Two Mommies* so kids with two moms would have a book that showed a family just like theirs.[12]

Heather Has Two Mommies was initially self-published, but ten years later, Alyson Wonderland, a small publishing house with the mission statement of "focus[ing] on books for and about the children of lesbian and gay parents," purchased it.[13] At that time it was widely distributed, but along with the wider audience came many challenges and attempts at censorship. In fact, it was the second most challenged book in 1994.

Interestingly enough, the only book with more challenges that year was *Daddy's Roommate* by Michael Willhoite. This title was another variation on a family setting, this one a divorced father whose life partner has moved in. It's a story that demonstrates a family consisting of two fathers doing typical family things. Most of the time, the public censorship of these books was at the hands of individuals, usually parents, who would take them from public libraries and then refuse to return the books. Occasionally, the challenge came from a school system, but these books were not normally included in school collections.

Over the next decade, more LGBTQAI+ books were written, primarily about families with two mothers or families with gay uncles, and mainstream publishers published few of them. Here are examples of published books that offered windows and mirrors for children in the ensuing years:

A Joyful Story Sharing LGBTQAI+ Ideals

Boy Meets Boy, written by David Levithan. Alfred A. Knopf, 2003.
Called by some a "gay utopia," this is the story of what life would be like at a school where everyone is gay, and that's just fine. There are normal teen issues but no angst about being gay. This delightful story is a great way to show that we may all be different but we are also the same.

A Gay Main Character Making a Life Choice

King and King, written by Linda de Haan and illustrated Stern Nijland. Tricycle Press, 2003.
This story finds the prince uninterested in the potential brides his mother parades by, as he has a prince in mind.

Based on a True Story

And Tango Makes Three, written by Justin Richardson and Peter Parnell and illustrated by Henry Cole. Little Simon, 2005.
This book is a new and different way to present gay parents based on a true event at a public zoo.

A Transgender Child

10,000 Dresses, written by Marcus Ewert and illustrated by Rex Ray. Triangle Square, 2008.
Bailey is a boy who dreams of dresses.

A Bisexual Character

Cut Both Ways, written by Carrie Mesrobian. HarperCollins, 2015.
This book is an authentic portrayal of a young man first realizing, and then coming to terms with, his bisexuality.

—— • ——

Finally, today, we are finding good-quality picture books written about a variety of family structures with which all children can identify.

Books for young adults have taken a similar path, one just as bumpy with many challenges and issues. Even before we had literature classified as YA, there was a novel, *Chocolates for Breakfast* by Pamela Moore, first published in 1956, whose thirteen-year-old main character had a crush on her female teacher and a relationship with a bisexual man. This eye-opening book dealt frankly with issues about questioning one's sexual identity during the coming-of-age years.

One of the first YA books to deal with gay identity and questioning was *I'll Get There. It Better Be Worth It.*, written by John Donovan, published in 1969 and rereleased in 2010 on its fortieth anniversary. One of the best-known and groundbreaking lesbian YA novels is *Annie on My Mind* by Nancy Garden, originally published in 1982. This book relates the story of two young women and the development of their relationship from friendship to something more, in spite of resistance from everyone.

Another book remembered by many gay readers and writers who were teens in the 1990s is *Entries from a Hot Pink Notebook* by Todd Brown. This title is told in first person by Ben, a fourteen-year-old boy who is trying to figure out the world around him and his place in it. His angst arises from breaking up with a girlfriend who loves him, losing his heart to a boy, and living a life of poverty. Because it is both humorous and realistic, this book reached many readers who were also trying to puzzle their way through their teen years.

It wasn't until 2008 that the first book about a transgender character, *Luna* by Julie Anne Peters, was published. Although he was called Liam by day, the main character did not really come alive until nighttime when he became Luna, decked out in beautiful dresses and makeup. Making the decision to share Luna with his family and friends comes about through a voyage of self-discovery.

Stories about characters within the spectrum of LGBTQAI+ continue to evolve and show a broader swath of gay characters, both primary and secondary. Sometimes transgender characters are the focus of the story and other times they are of lesser importance, but regardless, these stories all reveal the depth and variety of people and families today.

Rainbow Boys by Alex Sanchez, published in 2001, is the first of a series of books about high school boys who are frankly facing their homosexuality and everything that goes with it. AIDS, gay bashing, homophobia, and other topics are explored in this realistic fiction title. The characters in *Two Boys Kissing* by David Levithan, published in 2013, share a same-sex kiss, one that goes on and on, because they are trying to break the Guinness World Record.

The book is also notable because the story includes a chorus, not unlike a Greek chorus, that emerges periodically throughout the story. Consisting of all of the men who previously died of AIDS, the chorus talks about the way gay people have become more accepted and how many attitudes have changed. This book shares a heartfelt perspective and even a little history.

Published in 2015, *None of the Above* by I. W. Gregorio became the first book to deal directly with the issues surrounding intersex. Written by a doctor who also writes young adult literature, this story deals with a popular high school girl who seems to have everything, until after she and her boyfriend are crowned Homecoming King and Queen and the two attempt to consummate their relationship. Kristin feels so much pain they must stop. She visits her gynecologist and learns that she is intersex; while she looks and feels like a girl, she has male and female organs, each only partially formed. To make matters worse, she tells her best friend who then shares it with the entire school body through a text that goes viral, and Kristin's world comes crashing down around her. The rest of the book describes how she deals with this potentially life-changing event. Woven into the story is factual information about intersex organizations and medical treatments for intersex issues.

And a final book to consider is *Fun Home: A Family Tragicomic* by Alison Bechdel, published in 2007. This graphic novel is a memoir that details Bechdel's life from childhood through college. During this time, she navigates the twists and turns of realizing she is lesbian while being raised by her closeted gay father who runs the town funeral home. This is a unique recipe for a story, especially a true one, and it is told through a different format, that of a graphic novel. Even more interesting is that it was turned into a Broadway show.

DEALING WITH OBJECTIONS

As mentioned at the beginning of this chapter, homophobia is alive and well. Naidoo's definition of homophobia is "a societal belief that individuals who are gay, lesbian, bisexual, transgender, or queer/questioning are demented, evil, harmful to society, disgraceful, perverse, and otherwise unfit to live in society."[14] We are well into the twenty-first century and these messages, both subtle and overt, can be seen everywhere, from young children at play to politicians making laws and public policy. Though society has turned a corner in terms of acceptance and willingness to engage in dialogue, the backlash has been severe.

Though more common in the past, unfortunately, even now, children are often discouraged by teachers, librarians, and other professionals from discussing family situations and their own gender identities. Naidoo acknowledges that "children feel unimportant and invisible when they do not see representations of their lives and families in books,"[15] and other children aren't given the opportunity to explore and understand these issues in ways that will build empathy. As noted earlier in relation to the discussion with a fifth grade teacher about incorporating books on such topics in his classroom, it's not about the issue of sex (though with older students, it can be); it's about the issues of understanding, empathy, acceptance, and respecting basic human rights.

So if we agree that all children need exposure to LGBTQAI+ books and honest, open discussion, how do we deal with stakeholders who disagree? Here are our suggestions:

1. *Begin by taking a look at your collection, library, or classroom.* Does it contain a variety of fiction and nonfiction titles that explore LGBTQAI+ themes? Do you have titles with diverse secondary characters who offer a realistic mix of people one might expect to find in a group? Are there titles written on a variety of reading and interest levels? If your collection is genrefied, are these books blended in with their genres or do you have a separate section? Though there's validity to both approaches, we'd argue that unless you separate out books with topics related to other forms of diversity (race, ethnicity, class, age, etc.), then don't form a separate section for LGBTQAI+ books.

Also, have you collected the best titles? Have you consulted review and award lists? Have you read the books yourself? Do you have any anti-LGBTQAI+ books? Do you leave them in for balance? If so, like books that deal with diversity in other ways, be sure they are used in a manner that sparks conversation. How is this character portrayed? Is it an accurate picture? How should the author have rewritten that scene to make it more accurate? When weeding your collection, be sure to weigh the value of the book against its discriminatory content. And when purchasing new titles, be sure to consider only the best, in terms of both content and literary quality.

2. *Begin discussion with children as questions and comments arise.* Do you create a climate that fosters open discussion of ideas and acceptance of

differences in your library or classroom? Are you ready to guide a discussion that revolves around everyone, regardless of differences, being deserving of equitable treatment? We have found that one of the best ways to plant a seed is through a discussion of challenged and banned books. Christina teaches a lesson each year with eighth graders and their language arts teachers using picture books that have been banned or challenged for a variety of reasons. The hook with these books is that students remember them from their time in the elementary grades, and often they will rediscover an old favorite. Plus they are surprised, even shocked, that the titles have been challenged and are eager to learn the reasons why. The books she includes often vary each year, but one that is always included is *And Tango Makes Three* by Justin Richardson and Peter Parnell, with illustrations by Henry Cole. The discussion is always lively, and students extrapolate from the penguins' behavior to human interactions.

3. *Include outside stakeholders in the discussion when necessary.* We're always reluctant to give a heads-up to parents and other stakeholders about upcoming lessons and themes we're exploring in the library because it "alerts" them that there may be an issue, when there really isn't. Instead, if the talk is natural and all viewpoints are honored and openly aired, then it becomes part of the daily purpose and routine of education. Keep in mind that the issues truly at stake are those of basic human rights. At times, of course, administration, parents, or others do need to become part of the conversation. When? If a child gets upset, feeling as if he or she hasn't been heard, or any type of bullying becomes part of the scenario, others need to know. But this is really no different from any other discussion that includes topics related to diversity.

4. *Meet challenges head on, and never be afraid to explain your reasoning.* Remember, discussions around LGBTQAI+ topics are a matter of promoting basic human rights, as with any other form of diversity. Defend your choices of books by pointing to exemplary book reviews and suggested age/grade ranges. Verify that your library/school district has a plan in place for dealing with challenges, and make sure that it's followed.

A parent once questioned Christina's decision to share a picture book with first graders that, he argued, promoted cross-dressing. He went over her head, directly to the principal, who brought the complaint to her. Christina showed the principal the book, explained the lesson, and told her about the discussion. The principal defused the issue, and the parent was pacified. If Christina had the chance to relive that challenge, she would request to speak to the parent herself, hoping to not just pacify but encourage some understanding.

5. *Solicit allies when needed.* Why? For a couple of reasons: First, before an issue arises, having a common base of understanding, like-minded professionals can help bolster your convictions. Second, if and when a challenge arises, you have a ready base of professionals to turn to for support. Who? Seek out other librarians within and outside of your district or system and administrators at the building or district level. Another source of support is your state library organization, and if the issue is particularly prickly, you can contact the Intellectual Freedom Round Table of the American Library Association for advice and even legal support, if needed.

Librarians—school, public, and all other types—still face the stereotypes of being old-fashioned, out-of-date, and nonprofessional, when nothing could be further from the truth. We're truly a strong group of professionals who take our child patrons' needs and interests to heart and are willing to fight for them and their rights. It is our hope that the tools we include in this book will further your resolve to ask the questions that help promote understanding and empathy about LGBTQAI+ issues with all children at a time when it's crucially needed.

EMERGING AND CHANGING TERMS

So much has changed in our vocabulary over the past few years, including the transition from using the acronym GLBT to LGBTQAI+. The more accepted the community becomes, the greater the diversity in terminology, as people are able to be more open about and share their differences. This has resulted in more-complete definitions, as we move from simply using the terms *gay* or *straight* to *gay/lesbian* to *intersex* to *pansexual* and more; each term is acceptable and distinct. Instead of being overwhelming, this variety in terminology is our opportunity to allow for diversity in and individualization of gender identity.

For this book, we've chosen specific definitions for terms commonly used in the LGBTQAI+ community, according to the Human Rights Campaign and the University of California, Davis. As you read through this book's chapters and annotations, know that the following terms and definitions are the ones around which our discussions revolve. We acknowledge that there is no definitive or agreed-upon set of terms and definitions, and we are sensitive to that; we are choosing to be as inclusive as possible.

lesbian: A woman who is primarily attracted (emotionally, romantically, or sexually) to other women.[16]

gay: A person who is primarily attracted (emotionally, romantically, or sexually) to members of the same sex; though traditionally a man attracted to another man, this term can be used for any sex (e.g., gay man, gay woman, gay person).[17]

bisexual: A person who is attracted (emotionally, romantically, or sexually) to a person of the same gender identity/expression or to someone of a different gender identity/expression; also called "bi."[18]

transgender: A broad term commonly used for a person whose gender identity and/or expression is different from public expectations based on the sex the person was assigned at birth. Being transgender does not signify any specific sexual orientation; transgender people may identify as straight, gay, lesbian, bisexual, and so on.[19]

queer: An umbrella term sometimes used by LGBTQAI+ people to refer to the entire community; a term people often use to express fluid identities and orientations; often used interchangeably with "GLBT."[20]

asexual: Used to refer to a person who generally does not feel sexual attraction to or desire for any type of person. Asexuality is not the same as celibacy.[21]

intersex: Used to refer to a person whose sexual anatomy or chromosomes do not fit with the traditional features of "female" and "male," for example, a person born with both "female" and "male" anatomy (vagina and uterus, penis and testicles).[22]

Please see the glossary at the conclusion of this book for additional terms.

ABOUT THIS BOOK

The books selected for inclusion are quality pieces of literature and non-fiction, both factual and narrative, that have been crafted for children and young adults. They pass the literary tests for engaging stories and factual, intriguing nonfiction. Characters are realistic, settings are believable, even when they're imaginary, and the stories offer a wide variety of themes. The selected books create various moods and appeal to an array of age ranges from young children to young adults. Many of the books are new, ranging from the past few years to LGBTQAI+ classics that helped launch the topic in children's literature, often with considerable backlash.

For the reader's convenience, this book has been arranged into three chapters, with additional pieces. Following this introduction to the topic, complete with history, terms, and explanations, are these chapters:

1. Books and Conversation for Young Readers
2. Books and Conversation for Middle Grade Readers
3. Books and Conversation for Teen Readers

Included within each chapter are lists of exemplary titles that include annotations with the following parts: plot summary, comments on illustrations, and evaluation of content and back matter. Entries are listed by genre, including realistic fiction, fantasy, fractured folklore, historical fiction, and informational books. Within entries, each book is coded with one or more of the letters LGBTQAI+. Awards and honors (if any), conversation starters (i.e., discussion questions), and related resources are included for each book within the genre lists. Each chapter also includes a section with program, theme, and display ideas. Complete bibliographic information for the included titles appears at the end of each chapter.

We conclude with "Final Thoughts: It's about Basic Human Rights," where we hope to convince you of the crucial need to put our young patrons' needs first by sharing books of diversity of all types with all children. The book concludes with an appendix of additional resources, a more complete glossary of terms, and an index.

CONCLUSION

We are very happy to be bringing this book to you. We who work with children of all ages every day realize that they come from a variety of home structures, with a variety of backgrounds and experiences, and they all have unique feelings. We recognize the importance of books/literature being a window, door, or mirror for children—a place to see themselves, to find affirmation, comfort, and even security in knowing they are not alone. Our goal is to give you the tools necessary so that you can confidently share these books with the patrons you support.

Because of these reasons, we are sharing this work with you, professionals who work with children, whether as a public or school librarian, as a teacher, or in another educational capacity. We offer book titles for all levels of readers and introduce ways for you to happily and successfully share these books with your patrons, whether they are students, parents, administration, or other stakeholders. This is critical work we do, and the more tools we have, the better.

NOTES

1. Erin McClam, "Religious Freedom Restoration Act: What You Need to Know," NBC News, March 30, 2015, www.nbcnews.com/news/us-news/indiana-religious-freedom-law-what-you-need-know-n332491.

2. Dave Philipps, "North Carolina Bans Local Anti-Discrimination Policies," The New York Times, March 23, 2016, www.nytimes.com/2016/03/24/us/north-carolina-to-limit-bathroom-use-by-birth-gender.html?mcubz=0.

3. Nikki Grimes, untitled (address, Virginia Hamilton Conference, Kent, OH, April 8, 2016).

4. Margarita Engle, untitled (address, Virginia Hamilton Conference, Kent, OH, April 8, 2016).

5. Jason Reynolds, untitled (address, School Library Journal Day of Dialog, Chicago, IL, May 11, 2016).

6. Gene Luen Yang, untitled (address, Pickerington Teen Book Fest [PTBF], Pickering, OH, June 11, 2016).

7. Sadie Trombetta, "23 LGBTQ Books with a POC Protagonist, Because It's Time to Diversify Your Reading List," Bustle, April 27, 2016, www.bustle.com/articles/156314-23-lgbtq-books-with-a-poc-protagonist-because-its-time-to-diversify-your-reading-list.

8. Rudine Sims Bishop, excerpt from *Free Within Ourselves: The Development of African American Children's Literature* (Westport, CT: Greenwood, 2007), retrieved June 19, 2016, www.tumblr.com/search/rudine sims bishop.

9. Kelli Barhill, untitled (address, School Library Journal Day of Dialog, Chicago, IL, May 11, 2016).

10. "Jenny Lives with Eric and Martin," Wikipedia, last edited April 21, 2017, https://en.wikipedia.org/wiki/Jenny_Lives_with_Eric_and_Martin.

11. Rudine Sims Bishop, "Mirrors, Windows, and Sliding Glass Doors," *Perspectives: Choosing and Using Books for the Classroom* 6, no. 3 (Summer 1990).

12. Lesléa Newman, "Kids Books: Heather Has Two Mommies," LesleaKids.com, accessed June 10, 2016, www.lesleakids.com/heather.html.

13. "Abbot Young," JacketFlap.com, accessed June 20, 2016, www.jacketflap.com/alyson-wonderland-publisher-20112.

14. Jamie Campbell Naidoo, *Rainbow Family Collections: Selecting and Using Children's Books with Lesbian, Gay, Bisexual, Transgender, and Queer Content* (Santa Barbara, CA: Libraries Unlimited, 2012).

15. Ibid.

16. Human Rights Campaign, "Glossary of Terms," HRC.org, accessed May 28, 2016, www.hrc.org/resources/glossary-of-terms.

17. Ibid.

18. Ibid.

19. Ibid.

20. Lesbian, Gay, Bisexual, Transgender, Queer, Intersex, Asexual Resource Center. "LGBTQIA Resource Center Glossary," UCDavis.edu, accessed May 28, 2016, http://lgbtqia.ucdavis.edu/educated/glossary.html.

21. Ibid.

22. Ibid.

BIBLIOGRAPHY

Bechdel, Alison. *Fun Home: A Family Tragicomic*. New York: Houghton Mifflin, 2007.

Block, Francesca Lia. *Weetzie Bat*. New York: HarperCollins, 1989.

Bösche, Susanne. *Jenny Lives with Eric and Martin*. Illustrated by Andreas Hansen. London: Gay Men's Press, 1983.

Brown, Todd. D. *Entries from a Hot Pink Notebook*. New York: Washington Square Press, 1995.

de Haan, Linda. *King and King*. Illustrated by Stern Nijland. Berkeley, CA: Tricycle Press, 2003.

Donovan, John. *I'll Get There. It Better Be Worth the Trip*. New York: Harper and Row, 1969. Originally published in The Netherlands.

Ewert, Marcus. *10,000 Dresses*. Illustrated by Rex Ray. New York: Triangle Square, 2008.

Fox, Mem. *The Straight Line Wonder*. Illustrated by Marc Rosenthal. Greenvale, NY: Mondo, 1997.

Garden, Nancy. *Annie on My Mind*. New York: Farrar Straus Giroux, 1982.

Gregorio, I. W. *None of the Above*. New York: HarperCollins, 2015.

Koertge, Ron. *Arizona Kid*. New York: HarperCollins, 1989.

Leaf, Munro. *The Story of Ferdinand*. New York: Viking Press, 1936.

Levithan, David. *Boy Meets Boy*. New York: Alfred A. Knopf, 2003.

———. *Two Boys Kissing*. New York: Alfred A. Knopf, 2013.

Mesrobian, Carrie. *Cut Both Ways*. New York: HarperCollins, 2015.

Moore, Pamela. *Chocolates for Breakfast*. New York: Rinehart, 1956.

Newman, Lesléa. *Heather Has Two Mommies*. Illustrated by Diana Souza. Alyson Wonderland, 1989.

Peters, Julie Anne. *Luna*. New York: Little, Brown, 2004.

Richardson, Justin, and Peter Parnell. *And Tango Makes Three*. Illustrated by Henry Cole. New York: Little Simon, 2005.

Sanchez, Alex. *Rainbow Boys*. New York: Simon and Schuster, 2001.

Severance, Jane. *When Megan Went Away*. Illustrated by Tea Schook. Chapel Hill, NC: Lollipop Power, 1979.

Willhoite, Michael. *Daddy's Roommate*. New York: Alyson Wonderland, 1990.

Yang, Gene Luen. *American Born Chinese*. New York: First Second, 2006.

OTHER SOURCES CONSULTED

Human Rights Campaign. "Glossary of Terms." HRC.org. Accessed May 28, 2016. www .hrc.org/resources/glossary-of-terms.

Lesbian, Gay, Bisexual, Transgender, Queer, Intersex, Asexual Resource Center. "LGBTQIA Resource Center Glossary." UCDavis.edu. Accessed May 28, 2016. http:// lgbtqia.ucdavis.edu/educated/glossary.html.

MacDonald, Susan Peck. "The Erasure of Language." *College Composition and Communication* 58, no. 4 (2007): 585–625.

Norton, Judy. "Transchildren and the Discipline of Children's Literature." *The Lion and the Unicorn* 23, no. 3 (September 1999): 415–36.

Valentine, Colton. "10 Children's Books That Paved the Way for a New Queer Protagonist." *HuffPost*, updated May 28, 2015, www.huffingtonpost.com/2015/05/28/ lgbtq-childrens-books_n_7462250.html.

one

Books and Conversation for Young Readers

> *When I was child, my cousin Andrew was on his way to becoming a talented ballet dancer. Unfortunately, the very posh boys' private school he attended was full of idiots and bullies. One day a group of them grabbed Andrew's tights and ballet shoes and threw them into a tree where they dangled, mockingly, for days. He never danced again. This story was written in a rage at that memory. It's about being able to be different without being punished for it. Has the world changed since then? I doubt it, sadly. We are still made uncomfortable by those who refuse to live within our prescribed "straight" lines.*
>
> **–MEM FOX, ON THE REASON SHE WROTE *STRAIGHT LINE WONDER*[1]**

As revealed by Fox's quotation, children wrangle with issues of identity at a very young age. Yet many librarians and educators seem to feel that LGBTQAI+ topics aren't necessary in, and/or appropriate for, discussions with young children. They seem to think that these topics come to the fore in the middle grades or during the young adult years. We'd like to counter this argument with three assertions:

1. Discussions of basic human rights are never begun too early. We discuss fairness and equality, though not necessarily in those terms, as soon as children need to learn what they can and can't do or say—as soon as they start to become aware of others around them and realize that the world is not egocentric. Discussion is natural, as the occasion arises; so, too, is talk about LGBTQAI+ issues.
2. Children often have families that are not the standard pattern of one mother and one father. All family structures need to be validated, and many books in this age category do just that.

3. Children become aware of gender identity/expression at a very young age. They begin to identify with gender and to notice gender differences, and many of them experience a disconnect between what they feel and their biological orientation. The world around them, even before birth, begins to impose gender expectations. Children need to be allowed to express themselves as their inner selves demand. More and more authors and publishers have recently realized this and thus have begun to make available books that speak to gender identity/expression.

For all of these reasons, LGBTQAI+ books are needed for all children to read, listen to, and discuss. This chapter considers many titles—fiction and non-fiction, new and classic, although not the sum total of important books—that will help children see and understand both themselves and others.

REALISTIC FICTION

Baby's First Words, written and illustrated by Christiane Engel. Barefoot Books, 2017. (G)

This sweet little board book takes baby through the differing experiences of the day. From what the baby sees and hears upon awakening to the various feelings the baby expresses to the bedtime routine, this colorful tabbed book is filled with labeled objects and two obviously doting fathers. This is a valuable addition to the body of board books.

Conversation Starters
1. What does baby do all day? What do you do in a day?
2. With whom does baby share the day? With whom do you share your days? How do those people make you feel?

Resources
- Author-illustrator's official website: https://chengel.myportfolio.com
- Author-illustrator's official blog: http://christianeengel.blogspot.com

Charlie and Mouse, written by Laurel Snyder and illustrated by Emily Hughes. Chronicle Books, 2017. (G, T)

This early chapter book is a fun, engaging title that includes the daily antics of siblings Charlie and gender-ambiguous Mouse. Throughout the four chapters, they play together, romp throughout the neighborhood, and establish new bedtime rituals, while gay parents, Mr. Erik and Mr. Michael, provide loving support. Kid-friendly illustrations rendered in graphite and Photoshop are a fun addition.

Awards and Honors

- Starred reviews: *Kirkus Reviews*, February 15, 2017; *Publishers Weekly*, February 13, 2017

Conversation Starters

1. If you have siblings, what do you like to play with them? Do you create your own games?
2. Do other family members play along with you?
3. What are your favorite family activities?

Resources

- Author's official website: http://laurelsnyder.com
- Illustrator's official website: http://ehug.tumblr.com

Daddy, Papa, and Me and Mommy, Mama, and Me, written by Lesléa Newman and illustrated by Carol Thompson. Tricycle Press, 2009. (G, L)

These delightful companion board books for toddlers show a day in the life of the little one with either two mothers or two fathers. They are a joyous look at how each parent loves and cares for the child, and each shows a happy relationship between the parents. The text is simple, rhyming, and totally engaging; the illustrations are boldly colored, childlike paintings.

Toddlers will probably want to imitate some of the many appealing activities in which the families engage.

Awards and Honors

- Stonewall Honor Book, 2010

Conversation Starters

1. What are the children doing in the books? Who is with them?
2. Do you do any of these activities? With whom?
3. Who are the children's parents? Do they look happy or sad? Do the children look happy or sad? Why do you think they look this way?

Resources

- Author's official website: www.lesleakids.com

Daddy's Roommate, written and illustrated by Michael Willhoite. Alyson Wonderland, 1990. (G)

This is another classic LGBTQAI+ picture book with a simple, timeless theme. A boy's parents divorce and his father moves in with a roommate, Frank, and together the men create a loving second home for the boy. The story relates the many activities they engage in and shows how the two men truly care for each other and the boy. The illustrations are full-page color paintings in a realistic style, with a slightly animated twist.

Conversation Starters

1. How does the boy feel when his parents divorce and his dad leaves home?
2. How does he feel when he visits his dad's new home and meets Frank?
3. How do his feelings change as he gets to know Frank?
4. How do you feel as new people come into your life?

Resources

- Collection of resources about children's books: www.teachingbooks .net/tb.cgi?aid=17426

Dear Child, written by John Farrell and illustrated by Maurie J. Manning. Boyds Mills Press, 2008. (L)

This loving tale about the joy a child brings to a family is told as a story in verse, while the colorful illustrations depict the many day-to-day activities in which families engage: spending a day at the beach, shopping, napping, building a snowman, eating at a restaurant, celebrating a birthday, reading a story, and more. Three diverse families are shown separately, and together, enjoying family life. There's a single dad, an interracial couple, and a lesbian couple who adopted their daughter. This is a quiet and joyous story for very young children.

Conversation Starters

1. How does the story sound to your ears?
2. What do you think the families think of children? Do the families like the other families? How do you know?
3. How are the families different? Who is in your family?

Resources

- Author's website: www.johnfarrell.net
- Illustrator's website: http://mauriejmanning.com/portfolio.html

Donovan's Big Day, written by Lesléa Newman and illustrated by Mike Dutton. Tricycle Press, 2011. (L)

Young Donovan is so excited when he awakens; this is going to be a very special day. At his grandparents' home he prepares, including getting dressed in special clothes. He is taken to an unfamiliar venue to be part of his two mothers' wedding! The book is written in a positive tone and includes bright illustrations, so the reader understands that this is a joyous event. Donovan and everyone he encounters are truly happy.

Awards and Honors
- Finalist, Martin Luther King "Living the Dream" Book Award, 2013
- Rainbow Book List: Top Ten GLBTQ Books for Children and Teens, 2011–2016 (Commended, 2012)

Conversation Starters
1. Why would Donovan's mothers be getting married now?
2. Have you been a part of a wedding? How did that make you feel?
3. What is important about this day for Donovan?

Resources
- Author's official website: www.lesleakids.com
- Illustrator's official website: http://duttonart.net
- Collection of resources about children's books: www.teachingbooks .net/tb.cgi?tid=24252&a=1

Everywhere Babies, written by Susan Meyers and illustrated by Marla Frazee. Harcourt, 2001. (G, L)

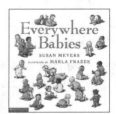

Beautifully done both through story and illustrations, this picture book is filled with action, as loving parents and caregivers tend to the needs of their little ones. The babies are engaged in nearly every activity available to them: eating, crying, sleeping, bathing, walking, playing, crawling, celebrating, and more. All sorts of parents, siblings, extended family members, and other caregivers are shown being busy, feeling tired, and loving their babies. The text is simple yet descriptive, and the illustrations, done in subdued colors, give a timeless feel to this treasure.

Awards and Honors

- Starred reviews: *Horn Book*, May 1, 2001; *Kirkus Reviews*, March 3, 2001; *Publishers Weekly*, March 19, 2001; and *School Library Journal*, May 1, 2001
- *School Library Journal* Best Book of the Year, 2001

Conversation Starters

1. Find the babies in the book. What are they doing?
2. How are the babies different?
3. Who are the adults with the babies? Are they happy or sad?
4. Who are the adults in your family?

Resources

- Author's official website: http://susanmeyers.com
- Illustrator's official website: http://marlafrazee.com

The Family Book, written and illustrated by Todd Parr. Megan Tingley Books, 2003. (G, L)

"There are lots of different ways to be a family. Your family is special no matter what kind it is. Love, Todd." This is the way the book ends. Leading up to that warm statement is a simple story told in simple language about all the many ways families are different, beautiful, quirky, and special. Parr also points out how families are alike: loving, hugging, missing members when they're gone. The vibrant, bold illustrations are rendered in childlike shapes on single-color backgrounds. The cover of a "family tree" will draw children in, and the story and illustrations will hold their interest.

Awards and Honors

- Oppenheim Toy Portfolio Best Book Award, 2004

Conversation Starters

1. What are some of the differences in the families in the book? What are some of the similarities? Which family is most like yours?

2. Why do you think the author and illustrator, Mr. Parr, used so many bright colors? Why are skin colors mostly different from real human and animal skin colors?

3. Can you draw a picture of your family using bright colors? Share it with your friend and compare how your two families are alike and different.

Resources

- Author-illustrator's official website: www.toddparr.com

A Family Is a Family Is a Family, written by Sam O'Leary and illustrated by Qin Leng. Groundwood Books, 2016. (G, L)

This quiet picture book features a diverse classroom of children sharing stories about their families, all very different. Lesbian, gay, single, multiracial, differently abled, and other parents are shown in a variety of activities with their children. The main character discovers that a family can be made up of anyone. The ink and digital, soft color illustrations are fun and whimsical.

Awards and Honors

- Starred reviews: *Kirkus Reviews*, July 15, 2016; *Publishers Weekly*, July 18, 2016; *School Library Journal*, October 1, 2016

Conversation Starters

1. Who is in your family? What do you do together?
2. How is your family like, or different from, the families in this book?
3. All families are different. Why is that all right?

Resources

- Author's official blog: http://123oleary.blogspot.com
- Illustrator's official website: http://qinleng.tumblr.com

The Flower Girl Wore Celery, written by Meryl G. Gordon and illustrated by Holly Clifton-Brown. Kar-Ben Publishing, 2016. (L)

Emma is thrilled to be asked to be the flower girl in her Aunt Hannah's wedding, but it's a little confusing. Her mother tells her she'll wear a celery dress and walk with a ring bearer. To her surprise, and relief, the dress doesn't have celery hanging off of it and the ring bearer isn't a bear, but a boy. Also surprising and delightful is that there are two brides being married at the synagogue. The colorful whimsical illustrations nicely complement the text.

Conversation Starters

1. How did Emma feel about being a flower girl throughout the book? How did she feel at the end?
2. Were you surprised that there were two brides?
3. Have you ever been in a wedding? Were you nervous, or did you have fun?

Resources

- Author's official website: http://merylgordon.com
- Illustrator's official website: http://hollycliftonbrown.co.uk

Heather Has Two Mommies, written by Lesléa Newman and illustrated by Diana Souza. Alyson Wonderland, 1989. (L, G)

Heather Has Two Mommies, written by Lesléa Newman and illustrated by Laura Cornell. Candlewick Press, 2015. (L, G)

This quiet, but groundbreaking story is a classic in LGBTQAI+ children's books. First written in 1979, republished in 1989, and published again in 2015 with new illustrations, this story of two women wanting to create a family is not outdated and completely usable today. Kate and Jane decide to have in vitro fertilization, and Heather is born. When she enters preschool, she discovers the wide array of family structures in which her classmates live. She's part of a loving family and an accepting world beyond. The soft pencil sketches and simple but matter-of-fact writing clearly tell the story of Heather's beginning, birth, and growth with honesty and joy.

Conversation Starters

1. How does Heather feel about her mommies?
2. How are the families of her friends different from hers? How do they feel about their families?
3. What kind of family structure do you have?

Resources

- Author's official website: www.lesleakids.com

Home at Last, written by Vera B. Williams and illustrated by Chris Raschka. HarperCollins, 2016. (G)

Lester, a boy who has been abandoned by his family, is adopted by gay fathers and is given all that he needs. He has to take time to adjust and learn to trust, but he does just that in this quiet, emotional story. The soft, abstract watercolor illustrations match the story for its reassuring tone and sense of resilience. An endnote explains that the story and rough pencil sketches were found after Williams's death, and Raschka turned the drawings into paintings.

Awards and Honors

- Starred reviews: *Publishers Weekly*, June 27, 2016; *School Library Journal* August 1, 2016

Conversation Starters

1. How does Lester feel at the beginning of the book?
2. How does he feel at the end?
3. What has happened to make his feelings change?

Resources

- Author's obituary: www.nytimes.com/2015/10/21/books/vera-b
  -williams-who-brought-the-working-class-to-childrens-books-dies-at-88
  .html?_r=0
- Illustrator's official website: www.sternnijland.nl/site_eng/koning
  .html

In Our Mothers' House, **written and illustrated by Patricia Polacco.**
Philomel, 2009. (L)

This is a loving, touching story of a family with two mothers. The illustrations are joyful indicators that a happy family comes in all forms. The three children are adopted and loved, and the family is accepted in this family-rich neighborhood, with one exception. This powerful story shows that positivity can win out over negative, narrow views. Share this book with families of young children to demonstrate life in a loving home of two parents. The illustrations are full of Polacco's recognizable faces; the book includes double-page spreads and images of a multicultural neighborhood.

Awards and Honors

- Notable Social Studies Trade Books for Young People, 2010

Conversation Starters

1. Look for the many different families in this story. What do you notice about them?
2. Talk about the things this family does throughout the year.
3. Why do you think one family chose not to attend the block party?

Resources

- Author-illustrator's official website: www.patriciapolacco.com

Jacob's New Dress, written by Sarah and Ian Hoffman and illustrated by Chris Case. Albert Whitman, 2014. (T)

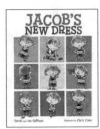

Jacob loves to play dress-up but wonders why he isn't allowed to wear a dress to school. He questions his parents, and eventually his mother relents, and Jacob and she sew a dress for school. Some kids poke fun, while others accept. The teacher explains that this is how Jacob is comfortable dressing and that girls at one time weren't allowed to wear pants. This picture book ends joyfully for Jacob.

Conversation Starters

1. What clothes make you feel comfortable? Are they different from what others wear?
2. Does it matter what we each choose to wear? Why or why not?
3. Was Jacob happy at the end? How do you know?

Resources

- Authors' official website: www.sarahandianhoffman.com

Molly's Family, written by Nancy Garden and illustrated by Sharon Wooding. Farrar Straus Giroux, 2004. (L)

Molly attends kindergarten, and her class is readying the room for Open School Night, when the teacher asks all the students to draw pictures of their families. When Molly includes Mommy and Mama Lu, she's told by another student that you can't have two mothers. Upon investigation of the other students' family pictures, the teacher points out that there are many different types of families and affirms each one. Molly questions her mothers that evening and learns that Mommy is her birth mother and Mama Lu is her adopted mother. She comes to terms with this and brings her family, including puppy Sam, to Open School Night. It becomes a joyous occasion for all. Written primarily in dialogue and illustrated in subdued, colored pencil drawings, this is a quiet, comforting book for young children.

Awards and Honors

- Capitol Choices Noteworthy Book for Children, 2004

Conversation Starters

1. Molly was proud of her family until Tommy questions her ability to have two mothers. How does she react?
2. How are the students' families different?
3. How is your family different from Molly's? How is it similar?

Resources

- Author's official website: http://nancygarden.com
- Illustrator's official website: www.sharonwooding.com/fineart/home.html

***Mom and Mum Are Getting Married!*, written by Ken Setterington and illustrated by Alice Priestley. Second Story Press, 2004. (L)**

Rosie is so happy; Mom and Mum are getting married. Rosie wants to be the flower girl, but her mothers aren't sure she's ready for it. This book reveals the joy in the celebration of becoming a family. The gentle illustrations depict smiling faces, reflecting the happiness of the day. Yes, Rosie does get to be the flower girl! This is a simple story to share with young children who will be attending a wedding, especially if it's for their own parents.

Conversation Starters

1. Why is this little girl so excited?
2. What members of her extended family attend the event?
3. What is the purpose of a ceremony?
4. Have you ever attended a wedding? Were you part of the wedding party?

Resources

- Illustrator's official website: http://alicepriestley.com

Monday Is One Day, written by Arthur A. Levine and illustrated by Julian Hector. Scholastic, 2011. (G, L)

This very simple text explains how children wait patiently day by day for Sunday. It shows ritual and tradition through the quality time each child gets to have with a parent on Sunday. The families are different and the activities they engage in are different, but the love is the same. The simple illustrations show a variety of parents—same sex, mixed race, heterosexual, and single—each demonstrating that all kinds of parents enjoy that special day with their child(ren). This is another good book for sharing with young children to demonstrate the normalcy of all types of families.

Awards and Honors

- Starred review: *Booklist*, February 1, 2011

Conversation Starters

1. Why are this father and son counting down days?
2. How many different families can you count?
3. What kinds of things do you do with your parents?

Resources

- Author's official website: http://arthuralevinebooks.com
- Illustrator's official website: http://julianhector.com

Morris Micklewhite and the Tangerine Dress, written by Christine Baldacchino and illustrated by Isabelle Malenfant. Groundwood Books, 2014. (G)

Morris is an imaginative little boy who loves to paint and try new clothes. He loves the tangerine dress in his classroom dress-up center, but when he wears it, the other children don't let him play with them in their spaceship. While being home sick for a day, Morris draws a picture of a spaceship and then takes it back to school where he builds his own spaceship. The other boys want to play in it as well, and by the time the adventure is over, they have decided it doesn't matter if Morris is in the tangerine dress or not. This book can serve as a gentle introduction to accepting differences in others, including students who may be transgender. The illustrations are subtle and softly colored, allowing the tangerine dress to be the focus of the pages.

Awards and Honors

- Starred review: *Kirkus Reviews*, April 15, 2014
- Stonewall Honor Book, 2015

Conversation Starters

1. Why do you think Morris likes to wear the tangerine dress? Does it matter to him? Should it matter to anyone else if he likes it?
2. Are there particular clothes you like to wear? How do they make you feel?
3. Why did the boys change their mind about Morris? What do you think they learned?

Resources

- Article and video: www.brainpickings.org/2014/12/17/morris-mickle white-and-the-tangerine-dress
- Website of recommended children's books: https://thereisabookforthat .com/tag/christine-baldacchino

Real Sisters Pretend, written by Megan Dowd Lambert and illustrated by Nicole Tadgell. Tilbury House, 2016. (L)

The brightly colored, action-packed illustrations, featuring a variety of layouts, set the stage for the daily life of two adopted sisters, Mia and Tayja, of different ethnicities. They, in conjunction with their lesbian mothers, go through the day, firmly establishing that they are a real family in every way. The speech bubbles add to the immediacy of this affirming story.

Awards and Honors

- Notable Social Studies Trade Books for Young People, 2017
- Center for the Study of Multicultural Children's Literature Best Books, 2016
- CCBC (Cooperative Children's Book Center) Choices, 2017

Conversation Starters

1. What makes people part of a family?
2. Are Mia and Tayja real sisters? Why or why not?
3. Who is part of your family, and why do you include them?

Resources

- Author's official website: http://megandowdlambert.com
- Illustrator's official blog: http://nicoletadgell.blogspot.com

Stella Brings the Family, written by Miriam B. Schiffer and illustrated by Holly Clifton-Brown. Chronicle Books, 2015. (G, L)

Young Stella has a problem: her class is having a Mother's Day celebration, but she has two fathers. Whom should she invite? After conversations with her classmates who have a variety of parents, Stella invites her entire family, including both fathers. The watercolor illustrations show warm happy faces and a welcoming classroom. This book serves as a gentle reminder to consider family dynamics when planning class activities.

Awards and Honors

- Starred reviews: *Library Media Connection*, December 1, 2015; *Publishers Weekly*, March 30, 2015

Conversation Starters

1. What is Stella's dilemma? Why is she feeling uncomfortable?
2. How did she solve her problem? What would you have done?

3. How would you feel if you thought your parents would not be invited to an event?
4. Who is the special person you would invite to a class function?

Resources

- Collection of resources about children's books: www.teachingbooks .net/tb.cgi?aid=24995
- Illustrator's official website: http://hollycliftonbrown.co.uk

---

A Tale of Two Daddies, written by Vanita Oelschlager and illustrated by Kristin Blackwood and Mike Blanc. VanitaBooks, 2010. (G)

This very simple story depicts two children on the school playground talking about their parents; the little girl has two daddies. As the little boy asks question after question about which parent helps her with various tasks, she answers which daddy it is, Poppa or Daddy. The dialogue clearly demonstrates the fact that between her two fathers she is well cared for. The illustrations are simple and bright, as is the message: she is loved.

Conversation Starters

1. How does the girl in the story feel about her family? Is she a happy or sad girl?
2. Look carefully at the pictures. What does each of the daddies do for her?
3. Who are the members of your family? Do they each have jobs as part of the family?

Resources

- Author's official website: http://vanitabooks.com
- Illustrator's official website: www.mikeblanc.com/illustration

A Tale of Two Mommies, written by Vanita Oelschlager and illustrated by Kristin Blackwood and Mike Blanc. VanitaBooks, 2011. (L)

Written in the same style as the previous book, *A Tale of Two Daddies*, this title shows three little boys on a beach talking about their parents. One child has two mothers and answers each question posed to him by sharing which mommy handles the task that needs to be done. The illustrations never show the faces of the mothers; because it is from the child's point of view, you see only up to their waists. The children's faces are bright and happy. Beautiful in its simplicity, this warm book is good for sharing with young children when discussing families.

Conversation Starters

1. How does the boy in the story feel about his family? Is he happy or sad? How do you know?
2. Look carefully at the pictures. What does each of the mommies do for him?
3. Who are the members of your family? Do they each have jobs as part of the family?

Resources

- Author's official website: http://vanitabooks.com
- Illustrator's official website: www.mikeblanc.com/illustration

This Day in June, written by Gayle E. Pitman, PhD, and illustrated by Kristyna Litten. Magination Press, 2014. (L, G, B, T, Q, A, I)

The very simple, yet powerful, rhyming text is the perfect hook for young listeners. With a reading or two, the children will be able to recite along with the reader. For the most part, the language chosen is readily accessible to primary grade children, but a few terms will need more discussion (see Conversation Starters). The spare text invites the reader to examine the illustrations, which are filled with a wide variety of people—young, old, costumed, ordinarily dressed, racially diverse, and transgender—and show many more ways to be distinct. The brightly colored, almost cartoon-like illustrations, both on the cover and within the pages, will draw children in immediately. The back matter includes a "Note to Parents and Caregivers" that helps explain the history of LGBTQAI+ and culture and how to share the book with children. Overall, this book reveals the epitome of joy for the very diverse group of characters—proud to be alive and proud to be themselves.

Awards and Honors

- Stonewall Book Award, 2015
- Notable Books for a Global Society Award, 2015

Conversation Starters

1. What do these words mean: chanting, clad, leather, sainting, tresses, and united? Which parts of the illustrations help explain these words?
2. Examine the illustrations with the children. Who are all the different characters? Are there dads, moms, children? What costumes do you see? What occupations do some of the costumes represent?
3. How are the characters feeling? Why?
4. Examine the signs the crowd members are holding. What do they mean?
5. What does the title mean? Why is this parade being held in June?

Resources

- Author's official website: www.gaylepitman.com
- Illustrator's official blog: http://kristynalitten.blogspot.com

FANTASY

Bunny Bear, written by Andrea L. Loney and illustrated by Carmen Saldana. Albert Whitman, 2017. (T)

This quiet story of anthropomorphized forest animals centers around a bear who feels more comfortable among rabbits, their lifestyles, and their homes. The other bears ridicule Bunny Bear for this, so he leaves the group, only to find Grizzlybun, a bunny who feels she is a bear. The other animals have a change of heart and accept both of the animals for who they are. The final humorous page is a spread of animals experimenting with other animal behaviors. The cartoon-like illustrations are just the right touch to this unique story.

Conversation Starters

1. Do you know people like Bunny Bear and Grizzlybun who don't feel on the inside the way they act on the outside? What do they say about themselves?
2. How do you feel about yourself? Are you accepted for who you are?
3. Whom could you talk to about this?

Resources

- Author's official website: http://andreajloney.com
- Illustrators' official website: www.carmensaldana.es

Families, Families, Families!, written by Suzanne Lang and illustrated by Max Lang. Random House, 2015. (G, L)

This book is told in very simple text that gently reveals different types of families. Each family is portrayed by a variety of animals, making all of the families accessible and engaging. In addition to traditional family groups, there are two roosters with a chick and two female koalas, along with grandparents raising children, adopted families, and stepfamilies. With its appealing photos, this book invites conversation between parent and child about the last line of the book: ". . . if you love each other, you are a family."

Awards and Honors

- Starred review: *Library Media Connection*, September 1, 2015

Conversation Starters

1. What makes a family?
2. How is your family like the ones in the book? How is it different?

3. Do you think the book is fun with animal characters, or would you like it better if they were human characters?

Resources

- Author's blog: https://suzannesmomsblog.com

***Introducing Teddy: A Gentle Story about Gender and Friendship*, written by Jessica Walton and illustrated by Dougal McPherson. Bloomsbury, 2016. (T)**

This soft, touching story (both through text and illustrations) begins on the cover and develops to the final page. The reader sees a frowning Thomas the Teddy peering into a mirror, and the reflection is a smiling Tilly the Teddy. The story relates a true friendship between Errol and Thomas, who worries that if he tells Errol he feels like a girl, Errol will break the friendship. Errol encourages now-Tilly to be herself and says he'll always be friends with her. They are joined by Amy and her robot friend, which she fashioned, and there's a lovely four-way friendship at the end. The soft ink and colored pencil illustrations are childlike and revealing of the true nature of the characters' feelings. The humans, Errol and Amy, are nonstereotypical, as the first is emotional and understanding and the second is spunky and mechanical.

Conversation Starters

1. Why does Teddy's reflection look different? Why is Teddy frowning? Why is the reflection smiling?
2. How do you feel about Errol? How do you feel about his friend Amy?
3. Do you like Tilly's photo at the end of the book? Why or why not?
4. If a friend of yours told you he or she didn't feel right about who he or she was, like Teddy did, how would you feel? What would you say? Would you still be friends? Why or why not?

Resources

- Author's official website: http://jessicawalton.com.au
- Illustrator's official website: www.mrdougal.com

Like Likes Like, **written and illustrated by Chris Raschka. Dorling Kindersley, 1999. (G, L)**

In ultra-simple, lyrical text and childlike, bold-color oil pastel and watercolor illustrations, Raschka presents a dejected cat observing paired off, male and female, animals, which leads to his feeling out of place and wandering away. To his delight, he finds another male who's a perfect fit, and they joyously bond. These somewhat anthropomorphized felines make a bold statement.

Conversation Starters

1. How does the white cat feel at the beginning of the book? How do you know? Why does he feel that way?
2. How does he feel at the end? How do you know? Why does he feel that way?
3. What changes his feelings?
4. What activities make you happy?

Resources

- Reading Rockets' author interview: www.readingrockets.org/books/interviews/raschka

Red: A Crayon's Story, **written and illustrated by Michael Hall. Greenwillow, 2015. (T, Q)**

Poor red crayon! He was red on the outside but blue on the inside. And no matter how hard he tried, he couldn't make his inside conform to the label on his outside. All of his friends and relatives had a theory as to what was wrong, and they tried all types of remedies. But a new friend requested he draw a blue ocean, and when he was successful, everyone saw him in a new light. The bold childlike illustrations, done in crayon and cut paper, with plenty of surrounding white space, will draw in any young child.

Awards and Honors

- Starred review: *Booklist*, February 1, 2015

Conversation Starters

1. All the other crayons' colors matched, inside and outside. Why do you think Red's didn't match?
2. Why did he try so hard to be red?
3. What did you think of the other crayons' trying to fix him?
4. Red found out that it's best to just be himself—blue. Do you try to be yourself or what others want you to be?

Resources

- Author-illustrator's official website: www.michaelhallstudio.com/pages/books/crayon/index.html

---

The Straight Line Wonder, written by Mem Fox and illustrated by Marc Rosenthal. Mondo, 1997. (G, L)

This is a classic piece by a classic writer. Fox begins with a trio of straight lines who are good friends because they are always the same. Then the first line decides it's boring to be straight and starts to jump, twirl, point, creep, and spring, much to the others' dismay. The second line exhorts it to be straight and then insists that "people will stare." But the first line doesn't care. It is soon discovered by a movie director and becomes the star of the show. Everyone loves its different take on life, and friendships are once again established. The cartoon-like illustrations are rendered in India ink and watercolor, and the font is large and bold.

Conversation Starters

1. Why do you think the first line decided to jump, twirl, point, creep, and spring?
2. Why do you think its friends didn't want it to?
3. Do you like to do things differently than your friends do sometimes?
4. How do you feel when your friends decide to do things differently than you do?

Resources

- Author's official website: http://memfox.com
- Illustrator's official website: www.marc-rosenthal.com
- Lesson plan ideas: http://aosa.org/lesson-ideas/straight-line-wonder-a
  -lesson-in-movement-and-writing

Worm Loves Worm, written by J. J. Austrian and illustrated by Mike Curato. Balzer and Bray, 2016. (G, L, I, A)

What happens when one worm falls in love with another? They want to get married, of course! But their friends have many questions, including "Which one of you is the bride?" and "Who will be the groom?" Even after the worms answer, the cricket says, "This isn't how it's always been done," to which worm answers, "Then we'll just change how it's done." This is a simply written, repetitive tale, told in engaging expressions, with a strong message: love is all that matters. Curato uses pencil and Photoshop to create the anthropomorphic animal characters, with plenty of white space around both the illustrations and text. One question we asked was "Why worms?" Because they are intersex animals that have the ability to reproduce by themselves but instead choose the love and companionship of another.

Awards and Honors

- Starred reviews: *Kirkus Reviews*, October 1, 2015; *Publishers Weekly*, October 5, 2015

Conversation Starters

1. Why do the friends have so many questions? What do you think of the worms' answers?
2. Why do you think the author and illustrator chose worms, instead of another, cuter animal?
3. What's your opinion about the ending?

Resources

- Author's official website: http://jjaustrian.com
- Illustrator's official website: www.mikecurato.com

FRACTURED FOLKLORE

King and King, written by Linda de Haan and illustrated by Stern Nijland. Tricycle Press, 2000. (G)

King and King and Family, written by Linda de Haan and illustrated by Stern Nijland. Tricycle Press, 2005. (G)

Folklore, especially fairy tales, is filled with sexist stereotypes. This tale breaks the mold when the queen mother insists that her son, the prince, marry and take over the kingdom so she can finally have time to herself. She calls all the eligible princesses she knows, but none makes a connection with the prince. One princess is accompanied by her brother, however, who results in the perfect mate. A wedding ensues, and all live happily ever after. The second book, *King and King and Family*, continues the tale as the two kings honeymoon in an exotic jungle and see how happy the animal families are. They discover a stowaway child in their luggage on the return trip home. They adopt the girl, and now the family includes Princess Daisy. The bold-colored, paper-cut, and mixed-media art creates exaggerated, childlike illustrations in both books that express the temperaments and emotions of the characters in these humorous but revealing stories.

Awards and Honors

- Starred review (*King and King*): *Kirkus Reviews*, February 1, 2002

Conversation Starters

1. What do you think of the queen's personality and how she treated the prince?
2. Did the ending surprise you? Why or why not?
3. Look carefully at the illustrations. Do you find them interesting? Point out details and express your opinion.

Resources

- Illustrator's official website: www.sternnijland.nl/site_eng/koning.html

HISTORICAL FICTION

***Happy Birthday, Alice Babette*, written by Monica Kulling and illustrated by Qin Leng. Groundwood Books, 2016. (L)**

Inspired by the life of Gertrude Stein and her forty-year companion Alice Tolkas, this gentle story of Gertrude trying to surprise Alice on her birthday is heart-warming. Alice thinks all her friends have forgotten, so she takes an adventure around Paris and encounters several delightful surprises. Meanwhile, Gertrude, a writer, but definitely not a cook, plans a special meal and a poem to share with Alice that evening. What ensues is a ruined meal that is saved by several friends arriving with gifts, as Gertrude writes a fine story of her cooking woes for Alice. Illustrations are rendered in soft pastel colors in a fun, breezy style.

Conversation Starters

1. Who was Gertrude Stein and what did she do?
2. Who was Alice Toklas and what did she do?
3. How do you think they felt about each other?
4. Did Gertrude's surprise for Alice work out as she wanted?
5. Have you ever tried to surprise someone? Did it work out well?

Resources

- Author's official website: www.monicakulling.com
- Illustrator's official website: http://qinleng.tumblr.com

INFORMATIONAL BOOKS

***And Tango Makes Three*, written by Justin Richardson and Peter Parnell and illustrated by Henry Cole. Simon and Schuster Books for Young Readers, 2005. (G)**

This is the famous true story of two male chinstrap penguins in the New York City Central Park Zoo. The zookeeper watched them care for each other over time and eventually found them trying to hatch a rock. He gave them an egg to hatch and raise, and they successfully did so. Families would come to the zoo to watch this amazing penguin family. Expressive illustrations extend this story so that children can understand the power of love.

Awards and Honors

- Starred reviews: *Booklist*, May 15, 2005; *Kirkus Reviews*, June 1, 2005; *Publishers Weekly*, June 16, 2005; *School Library Journal*, July 1, 2005
- Association for Library Service to Children's Notable Children's Book, 2006
- ASPCA (American Society for the Prevention of Cruelty to Animals) Henry Bergh Award, 2005

Conversation Starters

1. What can we learn about chinstrap penguins and how they mate? Where could we look?
2. Do male birds usually sit on eggs?
3. Do the penguins seem happy?

Resources

- Lesson plans: www.healthiersf.org/LGBTQ/InTheClassroom/docs/curriculum/Tango%20Makes%203_revised2.pdf

---

Gertrude Is Gertrude Is Gertrude Is Gertrude: And Gertrude Is Gertrude Stein, a Most Fabulous Writer Who Lived a Most Fabulous Life, written by Jonah Winter and illustrated by Calef Brown. Atheneum Books for Young Readers, 2009. (L)

The seemingly simple, repetitive text is packed with meaning, as was Stein's writing. Winter tells the story of Stein's adult life, writing, creativity, friendships with famous authors and artists, and her companionship with Alice in a style reminiscent of Stein's. Brown's childlike paintings are done in bold acrylic colors. Together, the story and illustrations make for an engaging story that

will get children talking. The back matter includes an author's note with additional information about Stein and how her work was often misunderstood in her lifetime but celebrated since.

Awards and Honors

- Starred reviews: *Bulletin of the Center for Children's Books*, January 1, 2009; *Kirkus Reviews*, January 1, 2009; *Publishers Weekly*, December 15, 2008
- Rainbow Book List, 2010

Conversation Starters

1. Why do you think the author wrote the story of Gertrude's life with so many repeating words? Share some of Stein's work with children, and ask the question again.
2. What did Gertrude accomplish in her life?
3. Who were her friends and special companion?
4. Why might Alice type Gertrude's writing for her?
5. Why do you think the illustrations are so colorful? Which is your favorite, and why?

Resources

- Author's official webpage: www.jonahwinter.com/gertrude.html
- Illustrator's official website: www.calefbrown.com

I Am Jazz, **written by Jessica Herthel and Jazz Jennings and illustrated by Shelagh McNicholas. Dial Books for Young Readers, 2014. (T)**

Simply told, this picture book biography shares the story of Jazz, a girl in a boy's body. She dresses like a girl and plays like a girl; it makes her happy. So when her supportive parents take her to doctors, they discover she is transgender. Her school accepts Jazz the way she is, and her friends love to include her in their  play. The upbeat illustrations, rendered in pastels, show a happy child when others accept her for who she is.

Conversation Starters

1. Does it make a difference what colors children choose to wear? Why or why not?
2. How do you choose your friends?

Resources

- Author's official website: www.jessicaherthel.com
- Illustrator's official website: www.shelaghmcnicholas.co.uk

---

***Keith Haring: The Boy Who Just Kept Drawing*, written by Kay A. Haring and illustrated by Robert Neubecker. Dial Books for Young Readers, 2017. (G)**

From the front cover sketch of Haring and one of his classic characters to the endpage drawings and the back cover that declares "Art Is for Everyone!" this picture book biography, written by Haring's sister, is testament to the joy Keith took in creating and sharing art. He was questioned throughout his childhood and young adult years about his work, in ways that were sometimes helpful and other times derogatory, but in either case, this spurred him on to create more. In New York City, he created his art in public places, and wherever he traveled, he invited others to join in and make art as communal as possible. An author's note shares more recollections about Keith, his childhood, demeanor, and generosity. Other final notes include additional information about Keith's life, passions, art, foundation, and AIDS-related death.

Conversation Starters

1. Look at some of Haring's art. What do you think of it? Could you draw in a similar style?
2. Why do you think people questioned his work? And why did he ignore them and keep working his own way?
3. What is AIDS? Learn more about it and how Haring's work has helped people prevent and overcome the syndrome.

Resources

- Author's official website: http://kayharing.com
- Illustrator's official website: http://neubecker.com/#!/image_23914

Martina and Chrissie: The Greatest Rivalry in the History of Sports, written by Phil Bildner and illustrated by Brett Helquist. Candlewick Press, 2017. (L)

This picture book biography is a frank look at both tennis players, who they were individually, their intense rivalry, and their close friendship. Bildner employs an engaging voice, sets their stories against the backdrop of the Cold War, and crafts the complex relationship between Martina and Chrissie. A concluding timeline adds additional information about their lives, including Martina's political defection, their careers playing doubles, and their partnerships after sports. The only place where the subject of Martina's lesbianism, and her activism for gay rights, enters the story is at the end of the timeline. Additional back matter includes a list of sources. The subdued color illustrations offer a variety of perspectives and plenty of action shots. However, some of the renderings of Chrissie and Martina appear to be a bit caricature-like.

Awards and Honors

- Starred review: *Booklist*, February 15, 2017

Conversation Starters

1. Do you like to play sports? If so, is there anyone who helps you succeed? Is there anyone who makes you a better player because he or she competes against you?
2. What were some of the differences in the two women's lives? Did those differences make their friendship stronger or weaker?
3. Do you think Martina and Chrissie were more friends or adversaries? Why?

Resources

- Author's official website: https://philbildner.com
- Illustrator's official website: www.bretthelquist.com

My Princess Boy: A Mom's Story about a Young Boy Who Loves to Dress Up, written by Cheryl Kilodavis and illustrated by Suzanne DeSimone. Aladdin, 2010. (T, A)

This true story is about a boy who loves pink, sparkles, and wearing dresses. He is loved by his family, even if some people question his choices. The illustrations depict faceless characters as a show of diversity support so that readers can impose the faces of their loved ones. While the text is simple, the message is powerful and should be shared.

Conversation Starters

1. Why do you think the characters have no faces?
2. Do you have any friends who dress differently than you do?
3. Would you like to have a friend like Princess Boy?

Resources

- Official website: http://myprincessboy.com

Rough, Tough Charley, written by Verla Kay and illustrated by Adam Gustavson. Tricycle Press, 2007. (T)

In fun, rhyming verse, the young reader is introduced to Charley Parkhurst, a young boy who was orphaned and eked out a living working for farmers and, later, as a steamboat hand and stagecoach driver. He's tough, he's rough, and he can handle any obstacle. Charley settles in the West, building a stagecoach stop and becoming an important, political member of the community. On his sick bed, it is discovered by a doctor that Charley is biologically female. A combination of a map, timeline, and fact boxes at the end tells Charley's story in more detail. The earth tone illustrations, representative of the mid-1800s, show the intensity and fortitude Charley displayed as well as his living conditions. Children will be enthralled with the action and pleasantly surprised at the ending. It's a must to share the back matter with children as well.

Awards and Honors

- Amelia Bloomer Project List (recommended feminist literature for young readers), 2008

Conversation Starters

1. Share with children a bit of what life was like in the western United States in the mid-1800s. In light of this, ask these questions: What were some of Charley's accomplishments? What do you think of them?
2. Why do you think Charley chose to dress and behave as a man? Were you surprised he was biologically a woman? Why or why not?
3. Do we all have the right to dress and behave in a manner that seems right for us? Why or why not?
4. How do the illustrations add to the story?

Resources

- Author's official website: www.verlakay.com
- Illustrator's official website: http://adamgustavson.com
- Collection of resources about children's books: www.teachingbooks .net/tb.cgi?tid=10533

Uncle Andy's: A Faabbbulous Visit with Andy Warhol, written and illustrated by James Warhola. G. P. Putnam's Sons, 2003. (G)

Beginning with an author's note about his relationship with his Uncle Andy, Warhol's art, and the time period of the 1950s and 1960s, Warhola sets the stage for the fun memories the story relates. When James was a child, he and his parents (Dad, a junk collector who designed art from scraps, was Uncle Andy's older brother) and his siblings would set off from Pittsburgh for unannounced visits to New York City to visit Warhol and James's grandmother. There were always so many fascinating things in Uncle Andy's apartment and his city. The time flew by as James studied all of Warhol's art, helped his uncle with his work, and was given encouragement by Warhol. Then Uncle Andy would send gifts and art supplies home with the family.

Though Warhol's sexuality isn't discussed, this would serve nicely as an introduction to Warhol, his life and work. The illustrations are richly detailed watercolor paintings that give the reader plenty to pour over and enjoy.

Awards and Honors

- Starred review: *Kirkus Reviews*, March 15, 2003

Conversation Starters

1. Which home would you find more fascinating, James's or Uncle Andy's? Why?
2. How do you think Uncle Andy feels when James and his family unexpectedly arrive?
3. Uncle Andy helps James with his art. Share some photographs of Andy Warhol and his art, and compare it with James Warhola and his art. How are they alike? How are they different?

Resources

- Author-illustrator's website: http://jameswarhola.com/index2.html

PROGRAM/THEME/DISPLAY IDEAS

All of the books in this chapter deal with family, friends, and finding your place in those circles. Most programing for young children includes a theme or unit about family, and these books should be included. It is entirely possible that you have a variety of family groups in your class or story time; and if you don't, that is all more reason to share the idea of a variety of families with your students. All families should be treated with respect and dignity, so thoughtfulness is required when speaking to and about families; not all students live in the stereotypical, heterosexual two-parent home.

Instead of celebrating Mother's Day or Father's Day, try observing holidays like Parent's Day or simply Family Day. Allow students to invite their caregiver(s), whether that person is a mother, father, grandparent, or someone else. Label the invitation "To the Person Who Cares for Me." Have children write or draw pictures of these people and their favorite family traditions to display. Perhaps you will discover some aspects or talents of the family members that they could then share with the group. Once the children understand the full range of family types, the talk becomes much more inclusive. Allow your students or story time children to spend time with and share conversation on these books about family. This is the best way for children to learn about similarities and to discover that the most important part of life, love, is a constant in all families.

CONCLUSION

As evidenced by the numerous books shared in this chapter, there are many excellent choices that deal with LGBTQAI+ issues on a primary grade level. Any or all would be acceptable to share with young children as you have conversations about similarities and differences, families and friends. We are all different in some ways and yet the same in others, and the uniqueness of each person should be celebrated.

The common thread in all of these books is that acceptance and caring are what matters. As we teach our children about fairness and equality, it is important to be sure we are unbiased in our presentations. Children are curious, and they will want to know why one friend's family is different from theirs. They have not been immune to the prejudice displayed around them, but they can still understand the rational explanation that differences are acceptable. Friends are to be gauged by the way they treat one another, not the way they look or dress.

Books like these should be available on classroom and library bookshelves and in your read-aloud stack. They will only deepen the understanding and empathy of your students for one another.

NOTE

1. Mem Fox, comments on *The Straight Line Wonder*, MemFox.com, January 9, 2013, http://memfox.com/gossip-behind-mems-books/the-straight-line -wonder-illustrated-by-marc-rosenthal/.

BIBLIOGRAPHY

Austrian, J. J. *Worm Loves Worm*. Illustrated by Mike Curato. New York: Balzer and Bray, 2016.

Baldacchino, Christine. *Morris Micklewhite and the Tangerine Dress*. Illustrated by Isabelle Malenfant. Toronto: Groundwood Books, 2014.

Bildner, Phil. *Martina and Chrissie: The Greatest Rivalry in the History of Sports*. Illustrated by Brett Helquist. Somerville, MA: Candlewick Press, 2017.

de Haan, Linda. *King and King*. Illustrated by Stern Nijland. Berkeley, CA: Tricycle Press, 2000.

———. *King and King and Family*. Illustrated by Stern Nijland. Berkeley, CA: Tricycle Press, 2005.

Engel, Christiane. *Baby's First Words*. Raleigh, NC: Barefoot Books, 2017.

Farrell, John. *Dear Child*. Illustrated by Maurie J. Manning. Honesdale, PA: Boyds Mills Press, 2008.

Fox, Mem. Comments on *The Straight Line Wonder*. MemFox.com, January 9, 2013. http://memfox.com/gossip-behind-mems-books/the-straight-line-wonder -illustrated-by-marc-rosenthal.

———. *The Straight Line Wonder*. Illustrated by Marc Rosenthal. Greenvale, NY: Mondo, 1997.

Garden, Nancy. *Molly's Family*. Illustrated by Sharon Wooding. New York: Farrar Straus Giroux, 2004.

Gordon, Meryl G. *The Flower Girl Wore Celery*. Illustrated by Holly Clifton-Brown. Minneapolis: Kar-Ben Publishing, 2016.

Hall, Michael. *Red: A Crayon's Story*. New York: Greenwillow Books, 2015.

Haring, Kay A. *Keith Haring: The Boy Who Just Kept Drawing*. Illustrated by Robert Neubecker. Dial Books for Young Readers, 2017.

Herthel, Jessica, and Jazz Jennings. *I Am Jazz*. Illustrated by Shelagh McNicholas. New York: Dial Books for Young Readers, 2014.

Hoffman, Sarah and Ian. *Jacob's New Dress*. Illustrated by Chris Case. Chicago: Albert Whitman, 2014.

Kay, Verla. *Rough, Tough Charley*. Illustrated by Adam Gustavson. Berkeley, CA: Tricycle Press, 2007.

Kilodavis, Cheryl. *My Princess Boy: A Mom's Story about a Young Boy Who Loves to Dress Up*. Illustrated by Suzanne DeSimone. New York: Aladdin, 2010.

Kulling, Monica. *Happy Birthday, Alice Babette*. Illustrated by Qin Leng. Toronto: Groundwood Books, 2016.

Lambert, Megan Dowd. *Real Sisters Pretend*. Illustrated by Nicole Tadgell. Thomaston, ME: Tilbury House, 2016.

Lang, Suzanne. *Families, Families, Families!* Illustrated by Max Lang. New York: Random House, 2015.

Levine, Arthur A. *Monday Is One Day*. Illustrated by Julian Hector. New York: Scholastic, 2011.

Loney, Andrea L. *Bunny Bear*. Illustrated by Carmen Saldana. Chicago: Albert Whitman, 2017.

Meyers, Susan. *Everywhere Babies*. Illustrated by Marla Frazee. San Diego, CA: Harcourt, 2001.

Newman, Lesléa. *Daddy, Papa, and Me*. Illustrated by Carol Thompson. Berkeley, CA: Tricycle Press, 2009.

———. *Donovan's Big Day*. Illustrated by Mike Dutton. Berkeley, CA: Tricycle Press, 2011.

———. *Heather Has Two Mommies*. Illustrated by Diana Souza. Boston: Alyson Wonderland, 1989.

———. *Heather Has Two Mommies*. Illustrated by Laura Cornell. Somerville, MA: Candlewick Press, 2015.

———. *Mommy, Mama, and Me*. Illustrated by Carol Thompson. Berkeley, CA: Tricycle Press, 2009.

Oelschlager, Vanita. *A Tale of Two Daddies*. Illustrated by Kristin Blackwood and Mike Blanc. Akron, OH: VanitaBooks, 2010.

———. *A Tale of Two Mommies*. Illustrated by Kristin Blackwood and Mike Blanc. Akron, OH: VanitaBooks, 2011.

O'Leary, Sam. *A Family Is a Family Is a Family*. Illustrated by Qin Leng. Toronto: Groundwood Books, 2016.

Parr, Todd. *The Family Book*. New York: Megan Tingley Books, 2003.

Pitman, Gayle E., PhD. *This Day in June*. Illustrated by Kristyna Litten. Washington, DC: Magination Press, 2014.

Polacco, Patricia. *In Our Mothers' House*. New York: Philomel, 2009.

Raschka, Chris. *Like Likes Like*. New York: Dorling Kindersley, 1999.

Richardson, Justin, and Peter Parnell. *And Tango Makes Three*. Illustrated by Henry Cole. New York: Simon and Schuster Books for Young Readers, 2005.

Schiffer, Miriam B. *Stella Brings the Family*. Illustrated by Holly Clifton-Brown. San Francisco: Chronicle Books, 2015.

Setterington, Ken. *Mom and Mum Are Getting Married!* Illustrated by Alice Priestley. Toronto: Second Story Press, 2004.

Snyder, Laurel. *Charlie and Mouse*. Illustrated by Emily Hughes. San Francisco: Chronicle Books, 2017.

Walton, Jessica. *Introducing Teddy: A Gentle Story about Gender and Friendship*. Illustrated by Dougal McPherson. New York: Bloomsbury, 2016.

Warhola, James. *Uncle Andy's: A Faabbbulous Visit with Andy Warhol*. New York: G. P. Putnam's Sons, 2003.

Willhoite, Michael. *Daddy's Roommate*. Boston: Alyson Wonderland, 1990.

Williams, Vera B. *Home at Last*. Illustrated by Chris Raschka. New York: HarperCollins, 2016.

Winter, Jonah. *Gertrude Is Gertrude Is Gertrude Is Gertrude: And Gertrude Is Gertrude Stein, a Most Fabulous Writer Who Lived a Most Fabulous Life*. Illustrated by Calef Brown. New York: Atheneum Books for Young Readers, 2009.

two

Books and Conversation for Middle Grade Readers

I said to myself, "I need to write a different reality for kids who are growing up gay." If I had grown up the way Joe is able to grow up in the world today—or the way I hope one day kids who are gay, or are whatever they are, will be able to grow up—I would have come to an understanding of who I was and been able to love myself and live free from fear, shame and self-hatred. That's where Joe came from.[1]

–JAMES HOWE (WHO CAME OUT AT FIFTY-ONE)

Middle grade readers very much straddle two worlds: one foot remains tentatively planted in childhood, while the other is reaching into the teen years. Much confusion can result from this, and a once self-assured child can now be insecure, moody, and/or rebellious. Educator-researchers Doubet and Hokett assert that an "'Under Construction!' . . . sign should be flashing above the head of every middle and high school student in our classrooms . . . [that] the degree of change experienced by the adolescent brain is matched only by that of the infant brain. . . . [They] often devote more time and energy to worrying about whether they are safe and accepted than to caring about whether they are learning."[2] Therefore, the assurance and understanding these books can offer are critical at this stage of development.

Therefore, LGBTQAI+ books for all middle grade children are necessary for the following reasons:

1. Growth and development explodes during this time period. As suggested by the previous quotation, middle grade readers can be consumed with the mental, emotional, and social environment around them and crave safety and assurance.
2. Families are still important, but more important is the exploration of identity. Middle grade children still cling to the support of the family, while simultaneously pushing authority figures away as they begin to think for themselves and develop an independent sense of self.
3. Relationship building with others outside of the family begins. Often, children's steps are tentative, as they reach beyond family boundaries and bring others, often with differing viewpoints and lifestyles, into their circle.
4. The need for a sense of safety and respect is crucial. And while all of this growth and development rages on, middle grade children scramble to cling to respectful, safe havens around them. These books can offer the understanding children need and the safe haven they deserve.

REALISTIC FICTION

Better Nate Than Ever, by Tim Federle. Simon and Schuster Books for Young Readers, 2013. (G)

Five, Six, Seven, Nate!, by Tim Federle. Simon and Schuster Books for Young Readers, 2014. (G)

This pair of middle grade novels is a smash hit, just like the main character, Nate. In the first title, we are introduced to Nate, a flamboyant actor-in-the-making who's been given a gift by his best friend, Libby. She's arranged for Nate to travel secretly from hometown Jankburg, Pennsylvania, to New York City for an audition for the musical *ET*. Through many travails, both hilarious and heart-wrenching, Nate's hard work and perseverance pay off. In the follow-up title, the reader is treated to Nate's unexpected performance, his awakening to his sexuality, and some unexpected friendships. For an added treat, listen to the audiobooks read by the author.

Awards and Honors

- Starred reviews: *Kirkus Reviews*, November 15, 2013 (*Five, Six, Seven, Nate!*); *Publisher's Weekly*, December 17, 2012 (*Better Nate Than Ever*) and November 4, 2013 (*Five, Six, Seven, Nate!*)
- Stonewall Book Award, 2014 (*Better Nate Than Ever*)

Conversation Starters

1. Describe Nate and Libby's friendship in the first book. How did that change in the second title?
2. How did Nate's family, both his parents and Aunt Heidi, support him?
3. Nate is becoming aware of his sexuality in the first book and gets his first kiss in the second book. What has he learned about himself?
4. If you could write a third book, would you have Nate back on Broadway? Would he and Jordan be dating?

Resources

- Author's official website: https://timfederle.com
- Video of author reading from *Better Nate Than Ever*: www.youtube.com/watch?v=PlYoSvmjUNI

A Boy Named Queen, by Sara Cassidy. Groundwood Books, 2016. (Q)

In fifth grade, Peter, self-nicknamed Queen, is the new boy at school, and he enjoys being himself, a little different from all the others. His clothes and interests are unique, and Evelyn admires these traits and slowly befriends him. He's badgered by many of his classmates but ignores their bullying. When Evelyn is the only fellow student he invites to his house for his birthday party, she gets a glimpse into what makes Queen tick. This short, quiet book, written with interesting Britishisms, allows plenty of room for discussion and discovery.

Awards and Honors

- Starred review: *Kirkus Reviews*, July 15, 2016

Conversation Starters

1. Does Queen feel comfortable with himself? Why or why not?
2. Why does it take Evelyn a while to befriend him?
3. How does Evelyn feel about Queen's family and home life?
4. What does Evelyn learn about herself?

Resources

- Author's official website: www.saracassidywriter.com

***Drama*, by Raina Telgemeier. Graphix, 2012. (G)**

Telgemeier's graphic novels, with their richly colored cartoonish drawings, fast-moving plot, snappy dialogue, and themes that reach their audience, are a staple in a middle grades collection. *Drama* introduces a gay character, Jesse, as the middle school students, led by main character/set designer Callie, prepare and present a production of the musical *Moon Over Mississippi*. Callie saves the set, as Jesse saves the final show, when the main female character is too distraught to perform the second half. There's plenty of drama on and off the stage, as the characters learn about themselves, one another, and the challenge of working together to create something larger than themselves.

Awards and Honors

- Starred reviews: *Booklist*, September 15, 2012; *Kirkus Reviews*, August 1, 2012; *Publishers Weekly*, June 4, 2012; *School Library Journal*, November 1, 2012
- Stonewall Honor Book, 2012

Conversation Starters

1. How are Jesse and Justin different and similar? Does each get to be himself? How?
2. What is Callie's reaction when parts of the musical production, and friendships, go wrong?
3. Do you find the ending satisfying and believable? Why or why not?

Resources

- Author's official website: http://goraina.com
- Book trailer: www.youtube.com/watch?v=ysWrqAMktc0

George, by Alex Gino. Scholastic Press, 2015. (G)

Stonewall Book Award–winning title *George* may well become a landmark title for middle grade readers. Gino expressly wrote the book for this age group because gender awareness begins very early and wasn't being adequately addressed. Third grader George has always known she was a girl, even though those around her insist on referring to her as a boy, especially her teacher, Mrs. Udell. When the class begins auditions for the play version of *Charlotte's Web*, George is denied the chance to audition for the part of Charlotte. Through a plot she and best friend, Kelly, devise, George not only plays the part brilliantly but lets her entire class know of her true identity. From the intriguing cover to the fun end pages to the engaging story told with large font and plenty of white space, George's introspective, honest voice comes through. Gino has included several everyday examples of gender stereotyping that readers will recognize.

Awards and Honors

- Starred reviews: *Booklist*, August 1, 2015; *Kirkus Reviews*, June 1, 2015; *Publishers Weekly*, May 11, 2015
- Stonewall Book Award, 2016

Conversation Starters

1. Why is George excluded from auditioning for the part of Charlotte? Is this fair? Why or why not?
2. How does George know she's a girl?
3. How do the adults behave around George? Mrs. Udell? Mom? What do their comments mean to George?

Resources

- Author's official website: www.alexgino.com
- News article and video: www.theguardian.com/childrens-books -site/2015/sep/09/alex-gino-george-transgender-protagonist-interview

Gracefully Grayson, by Ami Polonsky. Hyperion Books for Young Readers, 2014. (T)

Gracefully Grayson is an authentic, intimate, heart-wrenching story, told in first-person narrative, about a sixth grade boy who knows she is actually a girl. Grayson lives with her aunt and uncle and two male cousins because her parents were killed in a car accident when she was four. They are a kind family who treat her like one of their own, but Grayson knows she is different. She spends a lot of time in her room looking at herself in the full-length mirror and seeing her silky track pants transform into a skirt or a beautiful dress. At school things are different; she doesn't have any friends and eats by herself in the library. But the situation begins to change in sixth grade when Grayson learns about the upcoming school play. She auditions for the lead, a female role, and lands it. But this causes a huge ripple effect at school, affecting her English teacher, who is the play director, as well as Grayson herself. Throughout the rehearsal season, Grayson learns many things, about herself, about what makes a true friend, and even about her parents and how they feel about her longing to be a girl. This is a serious book that does a good job of sharing the emotional roller coaster a young person goes through when trying to hide his or her true self from the world, and the bravery it takes to finally show that person to all.

Conversation Starters

1. Do you have any friends like the ones in this story? Why or why not?
2. Why do you think the author wrote this book through Grayson's eyes?
3. How satisfied were you with the ending to this story?

Resources

- Author's official website: http://amipolonsky.com/about
- Summary and discussion guide: www.teachingbooks.net/media/pdf/ DisneyHyperion/Gracefully-Grayson-DG-FINAL.pdf

The Island of Beyond, by Elizabeth Atkinson. Carolrhoda Books, 2016. (G)

Martin likes video games, likes his mom, and likes to stay indoors. His dad, however, doesn't approve and thinks what Martin needs is a summer on the Island of Beyond, in Maine, owned by Martin's great-aunt, to toughen him up. After all, that's where Martin's dad lived and played each summer as a child. Martin is horrified to be marooned there and intends to hold his mom to her word about picking him up in a week. But his phone won't work on the island, his family's car breaks down, and he's forced to remain there. Martin decides he can't stay in the house all summer, ventures out, and meets Solo, the island wild child. They strike up an unexpected friendship, a potentially romantic one, as Martin teaches Solo to read and Solo teaches Martin to appreciate nature.

Conversation Starters

1. Why does Martin's dad want Martin to learn to be tough and more masculine?
2. What's his mother's role in his life?
3. What roles do Aunt Lenore, Uncle Ned, Tess, and Clam play in Martin's growth during the summer?
4. Why is Martin fascinated with Solo? What do they learn from each other?

Resources

- Author's official website: www.elizabethatkinson.com
- Book trailer: www.youtube.com/watch?v=3mCZGPj7WX0

Lily and Dunkin, by Donna Gephart. Delacorte Press, 2016. (T)

Two characters, Lily and Dunkin, have separate stories, yet they converge in a satisfying, meaningful way. Lily, whose birth name is Timothy, is entering eighth grade and grappling with knowing whether now is the time to show her true self. She has the support of her mother, sister, and best friend, but her father, terrified for her safety, and the bullies at school are leading her to rethink this decision.

Dunkin, aka Norbert, along with his mother, has just moved into the neighborhood with his feisty grandmother. Dunkin's father, who grappled with bipolar disorder, lost the family's savings on a failed business venture and then committed suicide, though Dunkin cannot yet come to terms with this. Dunkin, who struggles with the same issues, takes his first walk through the neighborhood after settling into his new home and meets Lily outside in her mother's dress. They reconnect in school, where Lily has decided not to dress as a girl yet, and strike up a tentative friendship. It's not always smooth, as Dunkin makes the basketball team, consisting of several of the bullies who torment Lily. Eventually, as both characters negotiate their individual struggles, they realize the value of their friendship and the support they can lend each other. Though Gephart is at times didactic, the story is an important one, with characters readers will truly care about.

Awards and Honors

- Starred reviews: *Booklist*, February 15, 2016; *School Library Connection*, August 1, 2016

Conversation Starters

1. Both Lily and Dunkin are grappling with their own issues, both personal and social. How does their friendship help them support each other? How do they let each other down?
2. How does Lily's family support her? How does Dunkin's family support him? What's the difference in the two families' approaches?
3. How would you have dealt with the basketball bullies if you were Lily? If you were Dunkin?

Resources

- Author's official website: www.donnagephart.com

***The Misadventures of the Fletcher Family*, by Dana Alison Levy. Delacorte Press, 2014. (G)**

***The Family Fletcher Takes Rock Island*, by Dana Alison Levy. Delacorte Press, 2016. (G)**

These two books are delightful family stories about four adopted, racially diverse brothers and their two dads. The first title relates a year in their lives, with each chapter focused on one boy, while still giving the reader a feel for whole-family dynamics. It's a new school year, with changes for all four boys as they face the joys and trials involved with this. The second title is a summertime adventure at Rock Island. Written in episodes, the story relates how the family, among other exploits, fights a racist real estate investor to help save a historic lighthouse. Levy writes in an engaging style that is both compassionate and humorous.

Awards and Honors

- Starred reviews: *Kirkus Reviews*, June 1, 2014 (*The Misadventures of the Fletcher Family*) and February 15, 2016 (*The Family Fletcher Takes Rock Island*); *School Library Journal*, June 1, 2014 (*The Misadventures of the Fletcher Family*) and April 1, 2016 (*The Family Fletcher Takes Rock Island*)

Conversation Starters

1. What does the Fletcher family look like? How does it compare with your family?
2. What are some of the changes happening in the Fletcher family? Do you have changes happening in your family? How do you deal with changes?
3. How does your family pull together when problems arise?

Resources

- Author's official website: http://danaalisonlevy.com

The Misfits, by James Howe. Atheneum, 2001. (G)

Four students, who call themselves the Gang of Five, have been friends for years and are now in seventh grade. They decide to attempt to change the bullying and name-calling environment at their school using the class election as their vehicle. They change the rules of the school's annual election by creating a third political party called "The No Name Party" to represent all of those students who have ever been called names or made to feel badly about themselves. While they ultimately don't win the election, they do spark some serious thinking about changes that should be made at school. These diverse characters are realistic and engaging, and students will see themselves represented here. This is the first book of several about these students: Skeezie Tookis, Addie Carle, Joe Bunch, and Bobby. Skeezie, who is also called Elvis, lives with his mom and sisters because of an absent father. Addie is the "too smart" kid who doesn't know when it's best not to talk. Bobby, who has a weight issue, lives with just his dad since his mom died, and works part-time at a local store selling ties. And then there's Joe, who is gay and trying to figure out just how that all works in middle school. They are great examples of how good friends are there for one another in the middle of the endless drama that is middle school.

Awards and Honors

- Starred reviews: *Booklist*, November 15, 2001; *VOYA* (*Voice of Youth Advocates*), December 1, 2001

Conversation Starters

1. It seems that while in middle school, everyone feels like they have something wrong with them. Do you ever feel like that? How do you handle it?
2. In the book, Addie chose not to say the Pledge of Allegiance, stating it was her right to choose. How would you draw attention to an issue with which you disagreed?
3. Imagine ten years have passed. Where do you think the Gang of Five is now? What is each character doing? Are they still close friends?

Resources

- Website for ideas that pair with the book: www.glsen.org/nonamecalling week

The Pants Project, by Cat Clarke. Sourcebooks Jabberwocky, 2017. (T)

Oftentimes, books about transgender children and teens center around transgender girls, but this one steps out of that box and focuses on a transgender boy, Liv. He hasn't come out yet to his two moms or new friends but is chafing over the dress code at his new middle school. Uniforms include skirts for girls and pants for boys, no exceptions. Liv navigates being a new student, finding new friends, and learning how to be himself in this restrictive situation. So he and his friends stage a day on which the girls wear pants and the boys wear skirts, resulting in the need for the administration to finally reconsider the dress code. In this story, told in a strong voice with natural narration, Clarke hits the vast range of middle school issues mixed with a multitude of different feelings.

Awards and Honors

- Starred review: *Kirkus Reviews*, February 15, 2017

Conversation Starters

1. Why do some schools have dress codes? Are they beneficial or detrimental?
2. Under what circumstances should a school make exceptions to dress codes?
3. Do you think Liv is a strong character to make a stand over what he believes?

Resources

- Author's official website: www.catclarke.com

Totally Joe, by James Howe. Simon and Schuster, 2005. (G)

Joe Bunch, whom we first met in *The Misfits*, was assigned to write his alphabiography, his life (all thirteen years of it!) in twenty-six letters. Although Joe has known he was gay and unique from a very young age, middle school is a new world. He still has his personal circle of friends, whom we also met in *The Misfits*, but as each of them is growing up and adjusting to adolescence, Joe faces many firsts, some wonderful, like a first boyfriend, and others, like his first breakup, not good at all. Along the way he "officially" comes out to his family and friends. The gang goes through their first experience of No Name-Calling Week, which realistically meets with varying levels of success. As Joe's autobiography progresses, we learn more about him and his place at home, at school, and in life. As one *Kirkus* reviewer said, just your "normal average seventh-grade homosexual."[3]

Awards and Honors

- Rainbow Book List, 2008

Conversation Starters

1. Why does Joe call himself "not your average Joe"? How do you think his teacher would respond to that comment?
2. In what ways do you think this is a realistic portrayal of being gay in middle school?
3. This story shares much optimism. Do you think that is truthful?

Resources

- Reading group guide: www.simonandschuster.com/books/Totally-Joe/James-Howe/The-Misfits/9780689839580/reading_group_guide
- Teaching Tolerance interview with James Howe: www.tolerance.org/magazine/number-29-spring-2006/feature/totally-james

---

We Are All Made of Molecules, by Susin Nielsen. Wendy Lamb Books, 2015. (G)

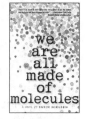

In this "not so typical" story about blended families, the reader meets Stewart, a thirteen-year genius, and Ashley, a fourteen-year-old popular girl. Through a story told in their alternating points of view, readers learn that Ashley's mother has married Stewart's father and they now live in Ashley's house. Ashley's father, who lives in the guest house in the backyard, is struggling with admitting he is gay. Interestingly, that is the secondary story line; the first is the challenge of high school with a new unusual brother that Ashley never wanted. Stewart has decided not to go back to the school for the gifted and is entering high school and public school for the first time. Poignant in places, humorous in others, this is an excellent story about accepting others and being yourself.

Awards and Honors

- Starred review: *Kirkus Reviews*, March 1, 2015

Conversation Starters

1. Many of the characters in this book are labeled. What do you think about labeling people? Have you ever been labeled?
2. Ashley's father lives in the guest house in the backyard. How does this add to the story?
3. This story is told by both Ashley and Stewart. What is the value of telling a story through two voices?
4. The characters in this book undergo many changes. Is that authentic?

Resources

- Author's official webpage: http://susinnielsen.com/books/we-are-all -made-of-molecules

FANTASY

Magnus Chase and the Gods of Asgard: The Sword of Summer, by Rick Riordan. Disney Hyperion, 2015. (G, T)

Magnus Chase and the Gods of Asgard: The Hammer of Thor, by Rick Riordan. Disney Hyperion, 2016. (G, T)

In *The Sword of Summer*, after his mother's death, Magnus is a homeless teen living on the streets of Boston, watched over by a male couple, who are also homeless. When he turns sixteen, an uncle breaks the news that he is a demigod, son of a shape-shifting Norse god, Loki. Magnus collects a magic sword from  the Charles River and is killed while using it in combat. He's taken to the Hotel Valhalla by a Valkyrie, where he meets a Muslim half-sibling, Sam.

As the second book, *The Hammer of Thor*, takes over, Magnus is allied with another half-sibling, gender-fluid Alex. The three of them are charged with obtaining the hammer that will save their father, Loki, from eternal torture. Concluding aids—glossary, pronunciation guide, and lists of the nine worlds and the runes encountered by the characters—are helpful. Both titles are filled with mythical allusions, action, adventure, magic, and plenty of sarcastic remarks sure to please middle grade readers.

Awards and Honors

- Stonewall Book Award, 2017 (*The Hammer of Thor*)

Conversation Starters

1. Riordan introduces diverse characters of other ethnicities beyond the European Norse characters. Why do you think he chose to do this?
2. He also introduces characters of diverse sexuality. Again, why do you think he chose to do this? Is he effective in creating believable characters?

Resources

- Author's official website: http://rickriordan.com

INFORMATIONAL BOOKS

Being Jazz: My Life as a (Transgender) Teen, **by Jazz Jennings. Crown Books, 2016. (T)**

Jazz Jennings tells her story of being a transgender teen in a highly honest, personal voice aimed at middle grade and older readers. She talks of her youngest years when she was sure of her female identity and her rebellion against gender stereotypes. Jazz writes of her middle grade years when she emerged publicly as herself and the strong support given by her family, especially her crusading mother. She also  takes the reader into her early teen years as she becomes a vocal activist for transgender rights. The concluding chapter is an interview with family members about Jazz's journey. Photos, both color and black and white, are interspersed throughout the book, and the back matter contains a lengthy section of valuable resources.

Awards and Honors

- Starred review: *Booklist* June 1, 2016

Conversation Starters

1. What were Jazz's feelings about her physical body as opposed to her gender identity as she grew older?
2. How did her family support her?
3. How did the community both support and oppose her journey?
4. What do you think Jazz's advice would be to a transgender child or teen?

Resources

- Author's YouTube site: www.youtube.com/user/jazzmergirl
- Author's website on transgender awareness: www.transkidspurple rainbow.org

---

Fabulous! A Portrait of Andy Warhol, by Bonnie Christensen. Henry Holt, 2011. (G)

Told in snippets of his life at different time periods through his success in New York City in 1966, the story of Warhol's life and art is revealed. Through straightforward, yet personal language and fabricated dialogue, middle grade readers will come to understand Warhol as a person and an artist. The illustrations, cover, and end pages, mimic and reproduce Warhol's style, while allowing the reader to understand the time period. The book ends with an author's note of additional information, a short bibliography, and an annotated timeline.

Awards and Honors

- Starred reviews: *Booklist*, June 1, 2011; *School Library Journal*, May 1, 2011

- Bank Street College Award, 2012
- Norman A. Sugarman Distinguished Biography List, 2012

Conversation Starters

1. Why do you think the author began at the end of her story (New York City, 1966) and jumped quickly to Warhol's childhood in the 1930s?
2. True biographies don't use invented dialogue. Why do you think the author chose to add dialogue to this book?
3. How do you think Warhol felt when he was bullied? How did he react?
4. Though the book doesn't mention Warhol's sexuality, it brings the openness and activism of the 1960s to life. Discussion of this time period would be an excellent background to his life and art.

Resources

- Author's official website: www.bonnietchristensen.com
- Collection of resources about children's books: www.teachingbooks .net/tb.cgi?aid=3815

Families, by Susan Kuklin. Hyperion Books for Children, 2006. (L, G)

Beginning with an author's note, explaining how both the text and the photographs were directed by the children interviewed, this visually appealing, inclusive book depicts a myriad of different family types and configurations. Included are quotations and photographs from today as well as of ancestors from the past. Each two-page spread expresses a distinct voice, with crisp, full-color photographs, as each child relates his or her individual and family stories.

Awards and Honors

- Association for Library Service to Children's Notable Children's Book, 2007
- Chicago Public Library Best of the Best Books, 2006
- CCBC (Cooperative Children's Book Center) Choices, 2006

Conversation Starters

1. How did the author-illustrator gather the information? What format did she use to share it with us? How does this make the writing effective?
2. Carefully look over the photographs of the families today. What do you notice about the makeup of each family? Consider such elements as these:
   a. Number of family members, both children and parents
   b. Ethnicities and genders
   c. Living conditions
   d. Emotions displayed

3. How does each of these reveal something about the families?
4. Look at the photos and captions of the ancestors. How do they help reveal the family's story?
5. Tell your family story.

Resources

- Author's official webpage: www.susankuklin.net/childrens-books/families

---

Pride: Celebrating Diversity and Community, by Robin Stevenson. Orca, 2016. (L, G, B, T, Q, A, I)

Stevenson, through bold, eye-catching, colorful photographs and the joyful story of the Pride movement, has created a title that is both enlightening and entertaining. Divided into four sections—The History of Pride, Pride and Identity, Celebrating Pride Today, and Pride Around the World—and filled with kid-friendly examples, this book will help children learn the overall story of the Pride movement. The book includes personal stories and back matter, including a glossary, references, index, and author's note.

Awards and Honors

- Stonewall Honor Book, 2017

Conversation Starters

1. What's the meaning of the word *pride*? How is the meaning the same, and different, in this book?
2. Who are the people who celebrate Pride Week? What are they proud of?
3. Are all people welcome in the celebration? Why?
4. What can you do to further understanding in others about the Pride movement?

Resources

- Author's official website: http://robinstevenson.com

Sex Is a Funny Word: A Book about Bodies, Feelings, and You, by Cory Silverberg and Fiona Smyth. Triangle Square Books for Young Readers, 2015. (L, G, B, T, Q, A, I)

This nonfiction title contains straightforward, honest information in a nonthreatening, bold-colored, graphic format. The reader is introduced initially to four characters of nondistinct gender/ethnic identities who relate the information through questions and answers. Blocks of information and drawings complete the relay of information. Included with the information is a discussion of emotions and support, with a complete atmosphere of acceptance. This unique book begins with a note to adults and finishes with a helpful glossary.

Awards and Honors

- Starred reviews: *Publishers Weekly*, June 22, 2015; *School Library Journal*, March 1, 2016
- Stonewall Honor Book, 2016

Conversation Starters

1. Whom do you think Zai, Cooper, Mimi, and Omar represent?
2. Have you had some of the same questions they have? Did their answers help you understand?
3. Whom could you turn to with further questions or for explanations of the information in this book?

Resources

- Author's official social media pages: www.facebook.com/whatmakes ababy and https://twitter.com/aboutsexuality
- Author's statement on family equality: www.familyequality.org/ _asset/nhswcw/Cory-Silverberg-Archieved-Spotlight.pdf

---

Who Is Elton John?, by Kirsten Anderson. Grosset and Dunlap, 2016. (G, B)

Told in an engaging, fast-moving narrative and illustrated in revealing pencil sketches, this look at John's life tells his whole story for middle grade readers. From his rocky childhood to the ups and downs in his career, to his drug dependency, to his bisexual life and his work for the AIDS movement, and, finally, to his marriage to Furnish and the birth of their two boys, this book offers readers a full picture of John's life and accomplishments. The book concludes with timelines of John's life and world events as well as a bibliography. This is a quality addition to informational books on LGTBQAI+ topics for this age group.

Conversation Starters

1. What were some of the obstacles John had to overcome, both in his childhood and in his adult years?
2. What are some of his accomplishments?
3. Describe his work for AIDS research. Was it important? Why or why not?
4. What is John's lasting legacy?

Resources

- Collection of resources about children's books: www.teachingbooks .net/tb.cgi?aid=27858
- Official Who Was book series website: www.whowasbookseries.com

PROGRAM/THEME/DISPLAY IDEAS

Planning an event or large-group activity can be a challenge. With students of this age, it is even more important to give them activities that make them feel safe and included. It is so easy for middle school students to imagine a slight or feel left out; egos are fragile and confidence can be easily lost. The middle grades can be such a polarizing time, as young people continue to discover who they are.

Set up stations where children can explore based on self-interest, not peers; a puzzle place or a coloring page station gives students a reason to work together even if there is no actual conversation taking place. Design your events to take all of this into consideration by always making sure to have available additional small activities geared around your theme, because some young people are more comfortable lingering around the fringes of an activity.

Creating an activity with an escape room theme is a great event for middle school students. While it is one large-group activity, you can create small groups that work together through a series of clues to "find their way" out of the library. Base the questions on your theme, like *Star Wars* or an upcoming author visit. Be sure to make the questions of varying levels of difficulty, and each should require more than one person to complete the task that goes with the clue. Your tasks should require different kinds of skills or strengths so that every person in the group has a chance to feel successful. To create your groups, you could select random names out of a hat, so no one is left out, or you might want to group the names by particular skills and then select one from each pile so that you get a variety of skills in each group. Remember that the object of this activity is to allow each participant to feel successful, so while there will be one winning team, be sure to plan a "celebration party" that all groups will be invited to join.

Escape Room Event Resources

- www.teenlibrariantoolbox.com/2016/07/tpib-locked-in-the-library
- www.breakoutedu.com

CONCLUSION

As you can see from this chapter's book lists and annotations, a common theme of these books for middle grade readers is emerging identity. Characters strive in a variety of ways, in various settings and under differing circumstances, to understand themselves and their sexuality. At the same time, these very characters hold close ties to family, still craving their love and support. The need for acceptance and understanding, by themselves, family members, and peers, is of utmost importance in this stage of children's development.

The titles we chose to include in this chapter are those we deem to be of high literary quality and informational value. Furthermore, we attempted to include a variety of genres to vary the perspectives of the characters and settings of the books. However, as will become even more prevalent in the next chapter for older readers, there's a preponderance of realistic fiction. We made certain to choose books that are developmentally appropriate for the maturity levels of the middle grade audience.

As with the titles chosen for younger readers, the books listed in this chapter need to be made available to all children. They validate individual emotions, actions, and thoughts while simultaneously encouraging understanding and compassion for others. For these reasons, they need to be in classrooms and libraries everywhere. Doubet and Hockett concur when they state that "in a novel, a historical account, or even certain textbook chapters, there are often a variety of perspectives represented. Only examining the text through all of these different lenses will produce a full understanding of it."[4] It's this variety of perspectives that all children need exposure to, and consideration of, in the hope that empathy will develop.

The kids from Howe's *The Misfits* have it figured out. Until the day comes when there is no more name-calling, let us hope that young people will find one another and form friendships that allow them mutual support:

> Kids who get called the worst names oftentimes find each other. That's how it was with us. Skeezie Tookis and Addie Carle and Joe Bunch and me. We call ourselves the Gang of Five, but there are only four of us. We do it to keep people on their toes. Make 'em wonder. Or maybe we do it because we figure that there's one more kid out there who's going to need a gang to be part of. A misfit, like us.[5]

NOTES

1. Tom Owens, "Totally James." *Teaching Tolerance*, no. 29 (Spring 2006), www.tolerance.org/magazine/number-29-spring-2006/feature/totally-james.
2. Kristina J. Doubet and Jessica A. Hockett, *Differentiation in Middle and High School: Strategies to Engage All Learners* (Alexandria, VA: ASCD, 2015), 9.
3. Kirkus Review, "*Totally Joe* by James Howe," *Kirkus Reviews*, posted May 20, 2010, www.kirkusreviews.com/book-reviews/james-howe/totally-joe.
4. Doubet and Hockett, *Differentiation in Middle and High School*, 182.
5. James Howe, *The Misfits* (New York: Atheneum, 2001), 13.

BIBLIOGRAPHY

Anderson, Kirsten. *Who Is Elton John?* New York: Grosset and Dunlap, 2016.

Atkinson, Elizabeth. *The Island of Beyond.* Minneapolis, MN: Carolrhoda Books, 2016.

Cassidy, Sara. *A Boy Named Queen.* Toronto, ON: Groundwood Books, 2016.

Christensen, Bonnie. *Fabulous! A Portrait of Andy Warhol.* New York: Henry Holt, 2011.

Clarke, Cat. *The Pants Project.* Naperville, IL: Sourcebooks Jabberwocky, 2017.

Doubet, Kristina J., and Jessica A. Hockett. *Differentiation in Middle and High School: Strategies to Engage All Learners.* Alexandria, VA: ASCD, 2015.

Federle, Tim. *Better Nate Than Ever.* New York: Simon and Schuster Books for Young Readers, 2013.

———. *Five, Six, Seven, Nate!* New York: Simon and Schuster Books for Young Readers, 2014.

Gephart, Donna. *Lily and Dunkin.* New York: Delacorte Press, 2016.

Gino, Alex. *George.* New York: Scholastic Press, 2015.

Howe, James. *The Misfits.* New York: Atheneum, 2001.

———. *Totally Joe.* Simon and Schuster, 2005.

Jennings, Jazz. *Being Jazz: My Life as a (Transgender) Teen.* New York: Crown Books, 2016.

Kuklin, Susan. *Families.* New York: Hyperion Books for Children, 2006.

Levy, Dana Alison. *The Family Fletcher Takes Rock Island.* New York: Delacorte Press, 2016.

———. *The Misadventures of the Fletcher Family.* New York: Delacorte Press, 2014.

Nielsen, Susin. *We Are All Made of Molecules.* New York: Wendy Lamb Books, 2015.

Polonsky, Ami. *Gracefully Grayson.* New York: Hyperion Books for Young Readers, 2014.

Riordan, Rick. *Magnus Chase and the Gods of Asgard: The Hammer of Thor.* New York: Disney Hyperion, 2016.

———. *Magnus Chase and the Gods of Asgard: The Sword of Summer.* New York: Disney Hyperion, 2015.

Silverberg, Cory, and Fiona Smyth. *Sex Is a Funny Word: A Book about Bodies, Feelings, and You.* New York: Triangle Square Books for Young Readers, 2015.

Stevenson, Robin. *Pride: Celebrating Diversity and Community.* Olympia, WA: Orca, 2016.

Telgemeier, Raina. *Drama.* New York: Graphix, 2012.

three

Books and Conversation for Teen Readers

"I guess people feared we were legitimising the gay lifestyle, and that in doing so, impressionable readers might become gay as a result." He laughs thinly. "I really wish I could write a novel that had that kind of power, but I'm not that good a writer. Besides, that suggestion is merely a sideways way of saying we don't want gay kids in our schools, rather than admitting that of course there are gay kids in our schools, and they deserve to be represented in literature."[1]

–DAVID LEVITHAN, ON HIS BOOK *BOY MEETS BOY*

eens have stepped outside of childhood and are reaching for adulthood. Their world is changing rapidly. High school presents even more academic, social, and identity issues. They are striving to discover who they are, while maintaining family and social connections and making decisions about their futures as they head into adulthood. Yet they are still dependent on their families financially and responsible for adhering to family rules and expectations. It's a confusing time, and teens are now, more than ever, ready to confront and reveal who they are.

Therefore, LGBTQAI+ books for all teen readers are necessary for the following reasons:

1. Search for identity is one of the strongest needs. Whether teens think they know themselves and are headed down a path of choice or are completely confused as to who they are, searching and questioning

are inevitable. Being able to explore others' lives vicariously is very important.

2. A sense of safety and the need for respect are crucial. Of all of the needs in Maslow's hierarchy, the sense of safety comes first for LGBTQAI+ teens, who are most frequently the target of bullying and at the greatest risk of suicide. Seeing the lives of others like themselves in books can be comforting and revealing and help teens to feel secure.

3. The need to be honest with themselves and the outside world is of great importance. The teen years are the time when many LGBTQAI+ members come out. If they have support around them, the transition is more stable. If not, it can be quite precarious. Books can be a source of enlightenment and stability.

4. Relationship building outside of the family is a main focus of development. Teens' lives are about connections and relationships and building a world outside of themselves. This is a scary time, as they decide what and who will be part of their futures. Books can provide a bridge.

5. A sense of fairness and justice is uppermost in teens' minds. The world still seems to be somewhat black and white, though shades of gray have started to seep in. Books can provide a host of situations, scenarios, and characters that teens can accept or reject, based on their values.

Young adults need tools for guidance: family, friends, teachers, counselors, and books, in addition to other resources. Fortunately, the wealth of LGBTQAI+ books that explore every facet of identity and relationships is exploding. Making the effort to find the right book for a young person at the time it is needed is an important job. Librarians and teachers need to know these titles and be ready to share them with teen patrons.

REALISTIC FICTION

Almost Perfect, by Brian Katcher. Ember, 2009. (T)

"Almost perfect" is the way to describe the relationship between Logan and Sage, the new girl in school, a tall, beautiful redhead. She had been homeschooled until this senior year. After Logan is dumped by his girlfriend of three years, he can't believe his luck when he begins to build a relationship with Sage. After their first kiss, Sage confesses she is a male. Logan is angry, thinking that when word gets out about this, that she is a male transitioning to female, people would think he is gay. We watch Logan work through anger and, finally, reach friendship. This story has its challenges. Sage's father is volatile, and Sage attempts suicide. Sage has to leave before the end of her senior year, so there is no "happy ending," but it is an authentic one. These characters are real, and the issues of being transgender hit home, which makes it a book many students will want to read.

Awards and Honors

* Stonewall Book Award, 2011

Conversation Starters

1. Have you ever thought about what it must be like to feel you are in the wrong body? How no one sees you for who you really are?
2. There are a number of pressures during senior year. How do Sage and Logan deal with them?
3. Do you know any transgender students at your school?

Resources

* Author's official webpage: http://briankatcher.com/site/books/book-reviews-almost-perfect

Annie on My Mind, by Nancy Garden. Farrar Straus and Giroux, 1982. (L)

In this groundbreaking novel, two teenage girls explore a new relationship. Liza is from the "right" side of town; her parents are both professionals and she is the student body president of her elite private school. She meets Annie, a girl from the other side of town, at an art museum. A friendship blossoms and soon turns to love. Neither girl expects this to happen, as they each had different goals. Over spring break, Liza house-sits for one of her teachers, who is in a committed lesbian relationship, and she and Annie spend that time together. An unexpected visit to the house by another teacher on staff reveals the girls and their relationship and also shines the light of discovery on the lesbian

couple, who are subsequently fired. In spite of this, they support the girls for a period of time. Liza eventually feels the need to push Annie away, and they go to college on opposite coasts. The book ends with Liza attempting to pen a letter to Annie, but she ends up calling her instead.

Awards and Honors

- Margaret A. Edwards Award, 2003

Conversation Starters

1. How did the differences in their schools, neighborhoods, and families influence the relationship between Liza and Annie?
2. How does Annie handle the guilt she feels about her sexuality? In what way does her relationship with Liza help her to see herself in a better light?
3. How have society's views of homosexuality changed since the book was published in 1981? What, if any, changes do you think are still needed?

Resources

- Author's official website: www.nancygarden.com

Arizona Kid, by Ron Koertge. Joy Street Books/Little Brown, 1988. (G)

This book was considered one of the best LGBTQAI+ books of the 1980s, both for its humor and its portrayal of a gay adult who is sexually active (and, of course, practicing safe sex) in the early days of AIDS. Billy, who is sixteen, is sent to Arizona to spend the summer with his gay uncle and to learn about veterinary medicine. By the end of summer, he learns not to judge people by stereotypes, experiences first love, and leaves  a larger man than the boy who arrived at the beginning of summer, even if he is no taller. This book, which is still in print twenty years later, was one of the few gay books available to young adults at that time.

Conversation Starters

1. Do you think that this book is still relevant today? Why or why not?
2. Who is your favorite character and why?
3. What do you know about AIDS? Is it still a major health risk?

Boy Meets Boy, by David Levithan. Alfred A. Knopf, 2003. (G)

What a happy, feel-good story this is! At this high school, sexuality in not an issue—students are out—and what ensues is regular high school drama. Boy gets boy; boy loses boy; boy wins boy back. Paul is a sophomore and Noah is the one he wins, loses, and wins again. This is a happy romantic comedy to be enjoyed by any and all teen readers. Also, that it was published in 2003 demonstrates the change in publishers' attitudes toward gay teen novels since the 1990s.

Awards and Honors

- Starred reviews: *Booklist*, August 1, 2003; *Bulletin of the Center for Children's Books*, September 1, 2003; *Library Media Connection*, March 1, 2004; *School Library Journal*, September 1, 2003; *VOYA* (Voice of Youth Advocates), October 1, 2003

Conversation Starters

1. This book was published over a decade ago. How do you think the events in this fictional high school match with your school climate?
2. Why do you think this book has been in print for so many years?
3. Do the characters in this story ring true to you? Explain your reasoning.

Resources

- Author's official website: www.davidlevithan.com

The Difference between You and Me, by Madeleine George. Viking Children's Books, 2012. (L)

"Sometimes you have to sacrifice something you love, if you don't want to lose everything you have." While this book doesn't have a happy ending, it is still a good choice for young people, especially for those wondering what it would be like to try to have a "secret" relationship in high school. The story is told in two voices, Jessie's and Emily's. The first is fiercely individual; for example, Jessie, whose  story is told in third person, is the only member of the "National Organization to Liberate All Weirdos." Emily, whose side of the story is told in first person, is the stereotypical popular girl and cheerleader with a boyfriend. Do total opposites attract? Not really, unless you count their "private time" on Tuesday afternoons. High school is a time for testing the waters, meeting and trying out friendships with different kinds of people, and while it doesn't always work out, experience is gained. For many readers, this is a safe and vicarious way to experiment.

Awards and Honors

- Starred reviews: *Publishers Weekly*, January 30, 2012; *School Library Journal*, June 1, 2012
- Kirkus Best Teen Books, 2012
- Rainbow Book List, 2013

Conversation Starters

1. What do you notice about the different groups of students at your school?
2. Which character do you like better, Jessie or Emily? How does the story being written from different points of view affect this?
3. Think about a time when you had to make a really tough decision about a friend. Do you think Jessie made the right decision?

Resources

- Author's official website: www.madeleinegeorge.com

Fat Angie, by e. E. Charlton-Trujillo. Candlewick Press, 2013. (L)

Angie's weight problems are symptomatic of several emotional issues: a star basketball player sister who goes missing during a battle in Afghanistan, a workaholic lawyer mother, and a miserable adopted Korean brother. She cries out for help in many ways, including cutting herself; but then KC walks into her life. New, cool, and edgy, KC turns Angie's world upside down. Finally, Angie decides she's going to try out for the basketball team to follow in her sister's footsteps. Through conditioning, KC's love and support, and eventually the support of her neighbors, Angie embarks on her path to wellness, both mental and physical.

Awards and Honors

- Starred reviews: *Publishers Weekly*, January 14, 2013; *School Library Journal*, May 1, 2013
- Stonewall Book Award, 2014

Conversation Starters

1. Angie's neighbor and "friend" Jake seems to be her only ally at school and in the neighborhood before KC arrives. How and why does his role change?
2. What part does KC play in Angie's life? Is she "too good to be true"? What are KC's issues? What part does Angie play in KC's life?

Resources

- Author's official website: http://bigdreamswrite.com

Georgia Peaches and Other Forbidden Fruit, by Jaye Robin Brown. HarperTeen, 2016. (L)

Joanna Gordon has agreed to help her dad, a radio evangelist, by "laying low" for her senior year, when they move to a rural part of Georgia from Atlanta to be near his third wife's family. This means not being her true lesbian self.

And the reward? Next summer, travel and fun with her best friend, Dana. Joanna also sees this as an opportunity to possibly land a teen ministry on her dad's show. But it's harder to suppress her true self than she thought, especially when she meets Mary Carlson, local schoolmate and churchgoer. As a more-than-friendship may be developing, Joanna becomes conflicted as to how and when to come out, not risk this new friendship, not break the deal with her father, and not give up the teen ministry. The reader will be won over by Joanna's engaging, snarky voice and attitude and drawn into her dilemma.

Awards and Honors

- Starred reviews: *Kirkus Reviews*, June 15, 2016; *Publishers Weekly*, May 23, 2016; *School Library Journal*, August 1, 2016

Conversation Starters

1. Why did Joanna agree to hide her true self for a year? Would you have done the same? Why or why not?
2. Think about the way Joanna handled the development of a relationship with Mary Carlson. Who did she hurt? Would there have been a better way to handle it?
3. Was Joanna's father being fair? What do you think about his reactions?
4. How did the relationship between Joanna and her father's third wife change? Was it realistic? Why or why not?

Resources

- Author's official website: www.jayerobinbrown.com

The Great American Whatever, by Tim Federle. Simon and Schuster, 2016. (G)

What's Federle's forte? Acting, theater, and movies, of course. And Federle's first step into young adult literature is told with both angst and humor. Enter Quinn, a teenager who's attempting to write a Hollywood screenplay. But his sister's death and the emotional withdrawal of his mother have made him a recluse and stifled his writing abilities.

Enter Geoff, a friend, who drags Quinn out of his cocoon and to a college party, where Quinn meets a hot boy, Amir. Through these connections, Quinn starts to emerge again as the star of his own life, reclaim his value, and begin writing again. Though Federle hits the middle school audience more closely with his Nate series, Quinn will resonate with today's teens.

Awards and Honors

- Starred reviews: *Booklist*, December 1, 2015; *Kirkus Reviews*, December 15, 2015; *School Library Journal*, January 1, 2016
- Rainbow Book List, 2017

Conversation Starters

1. Quinn's creative outlet is screenplay writing. Does that seem to help him keep his life's focus? What's your creative outlet?
2. How do others in his life function to help Quinn define himself? His mother? Geoff? Amir?
3. Have you read Federle's Nate books? If so, which series do you think is more effective for the intended audience?

Resources

- Author's video clip: www.youtube.com/watch?v=Qg1f1rlYBFk
- Author's official website: https://timfederle.com

Hard Love, by Ellen Wittlinger. Simon and Schuster, 1999. (L)

The first to explore a young man falling for a lesbian, this book tells the story of Jon "Gio" Galardi, a disenfranchised young man. His parents have divorced and neither spares any emotion for him, so Jon decides not to have any himself, not to feel anything. A loner with only one sort-of friend at school, Jon turns to writing to try to express what he feels. He discovers zines as a way to test his writing prowess and begins to follow other writers. Enter Marisol Guzman, self-proclaimed "Puerto Rican Cuban Yankee Lesbian." Jon is taken by her writing and manages to meet her, she nicknames him Gio, and their friendship begins. She is another lone duck. As the story progresses, we witness "Gio" fall for

Marisol, and our hearts ache even as we read because we know this is not going to be a story with a happy ending. It is an authentic ending, however. Because this story was published in 1999, it was a groundbreaking attempt to explore these feelings in a book for young people.

Awards and Honors

- Starred reviews: *Booklist*, October 1, 1999; *KLIATT*, May 1, 2001; *School Library Journal*, July 1, 1999
- Michael L. Printz Award, Honor Book, 2000

Conversation Starters

1. Do you ever feel like one of the loners at school? How do you handle that?
2. In what way does writing help with feelings? Or why doesn't it?
3. How do you think you would handle Gio's situation?

Resources

- Author's official webpage: www.ellenwittlinger.com/hardlove.html

---

Highly Illogical Behavior, by John Corey Whaley. Dial Books, 2016. (G)

Solomon is an agoraphobic, and Lisa is a determined psychology student who wants to write the most convincing college scholarship essay ever. Put the two together, and what starts out as a project ends as an unlikely friendship. Solomon is plagued with panic attacks, and his parents allow him to be homeschooled. Lisa is overzealous and sees Solomon as a humanitarian project, with unexpected  consequences. Solomon falls for Lisa's friend Clark, making for a tender relationship. Through this story told from two points of view in a reporter-like tone, the reader gets an inside look at both lives and will come to care deeply about each character.

Awards and Honors

- Starred reviews: *Kirkus Reviews*, February 15, 2016; *Publishers Weekly*, February 29, 2016; *School Library Journal*, April 1, 2016; *VOYA* (*Voice of Youth Advocates*), June 1, 2016

Conversation Starters

1. Is what Lisa is doing ethical? Why or why not?
2. Considering the outcomes of her study, were the risks she took worth it? Defend your answer.
3. Which character do you care the most about? Why?

Resources

- Author's official website: http://johncoreywhaley.com
- YALSA's author interview: www.yalsa.ala.org/thehub/2012/01/12/author-interview-john-corey-whaley

---

History Is All You Left Me, by Adam Silvera. Soho Teen, 2017. (G)

The story opens with Griffin caving in emotionally at the funeral of his ex-boyfriend, Theo, who died from a drowning accident. Even though Theo had moved, begun college, and was now dating another boy, Griffin had always believed the two of them would eventually be together. The only one Griffin now has to confide in is Jackson, but even with his support, Griffin, who suffers from obsessive-compulsive disorder, spirals downward. Through a story told in chapters that alternate between present-day Griffin and his past with Theo, it's obvious their relationship was very tender, and the presence of Theo is palpable. There's a gap in the two time periods—a story not yet revealed—that is slowly closed as the book progresses.

Awards and Honors

- Starred reviews: *Booklist*, October 1, 2016; *Kirkus Reviews*, October 15, 2016; *Publishers Weekly*, October 31, 2016; *School Library Journal*, November 1, 2016

Conversation Starters

1. How does the format of juxtaposing past and present work for this story? Or doesn't it? Why or why not?
2. How do you see Griffin and Theo's relationship? Griffin and Jackson's?
3. Will Griffin overcome and prevail? Defend your answer.

Resources

- Author's official website: www.adamsilvera.com

I Am J, by Cris Beam. Little, Brown, 2011. (T)

J is a young person in transition, from childhood to young adult to adult. In addition, he transitions from girl to boy. J knew from a young age he was a boy trapped in a girl's body, and that only got worse when puberty commenced. J's mother seems to have accepted J as a lesbian but not as a transgender teen. After J loses the friendship of his friend Melissa, for whom he really has romantic feelings, J eventually runs away and enrolls in a school for gay and transgender teens. There he does make friends and learns about hormone therapy. At eighteen, he begins the transformation, after which he manages to go to college and study photography. (The author, Cris Beam, has also written an adult informational book, *Transparent: Love, Family and Living the T with Transgender Teenagers*.) The primary characters are authentic, and the secondary characters are carefully placed to further the development of J. This is a well-written story to share with teens.

Awards and Honors

- Starred reviews: *Booklist*, December 1, 2010; *Bulletin of the Center for Children's Books*, February 1, 2011; *Kirkus Reviews*, February 1, 2011

Conversation Starters

1. Do you have any friends who identify as transgender? Once they "came out," did it change how you interacted with them?

2. In what way do you think the characters of this book are authentic? Does anyone behave in a way you think is not authentic?

3. Why do you think J's mother accepted him as a lesbian but not as transgender?

Resources

- Author's official website: www.crisbeam.com

If I Was Your Girl, by Meredith Russo. Flatiron Books, 2016. (T)

For her senior year, Amanda decides to uproot herself and relocate to her father's home in Tennessee, even though her father walked out on her mother years ago. Why did she do this? Because she's transgender and has been bullied and injured at her school and in her community. Amanda decides to lay low and not get close to anyone for the year, but then she falls for Grant and wants to risk it all by sharing her past life as Andrew, which is done through flashbacks. Her relationship with her father is slowly mended as Amanda comes to realize he's truly afraid for her life. Honest and contemplative, this story is authored by a transgendered woman.

Awards and Honors

- Starred reviews: *Kirkus Reviews*, March 15, 2016; *Publishers Weekly*, March 7, 2016; *VOYA (Voice of Youth Advocates)*, June 1, 2016
- YALSA's Best Fiction for Young Adults, 2017
- Stonewall Book Award, 2017
- YALSA's Top Ten Quick Picks for Reluctant Young Adult Readers, 2017

Conversation Starters

1. Which was more of a risk: Amanda remaining with her mother or her choosing to relocate to her father's home? Why?

2. Was revealing her past to Grant a choice you would have made? Why or why not?

3. How do you feel about Amanda's father, both in the past and by the end of the book?

Resources

- Author interview: www.gayya.org/2016/11/interview-meredith-russo
  -author-of-if-i-was-your-girl

The Inexplicable Logic of My Life, by Benjamin Alire Saenz. Clarion Books, 2017. (G)

Saenz has created characters, voices, relationships, situations, themes, and words of wisdom that will not soon be forgotten by the reader. Salvador (Sal), adopted by his gay father, Vincente, after his mother's death when he was three, lives a life of stability and happiness in a very nurturing family. He is joined by his best friend, Samantha (Sam), who's the adult in her family, which includes her hard-drinking mother; and Fito, a gay, nearly homeless boy, makes the friendship a trio. This is senior year for them, and Sal is worrying about college next year, and his beloved grandmother, Mima, is dying from cancer. To further complicate the year, Sam is adopted by Vincente when her mother is killed in a car accident. The circle is tightened after the trauma as Sam and Sal come to accept a former boyfriend of Vincente's back into their lives. The short chapters are told in a melodic rhythm, filled with deeply emotional phrases that cut to the heart of the characters' joy and turmoil. These complex characters live out themes of love, family, friendship, sexuality, health, death, responsibility, the future, and more.

Awards and Honors

- Starred reviews: *Kirkus Reviews,* December 15, 2016; *Publishers Weekly,* January 2, 2017; *School Library Journal,* January 1, 2017; *VOYA (Voice of Youth Advocates),* April 1, 2017

Conversation Starters

1. Do you think the families represented (Sal and Vincente and Sam and her mother) are realistic? Why or why not?
2. Think about the friendships, both longstanding and new, in this story. Are they realistic? Why or why not?
3. There are many memorable, meaningful phrases in this book. Find one that speaks to you and share it with a friend.

Resources

- Author interview: www.hbook.com/2017/03/authors-illustrators/
benjamin-alire-saenz-talks-with-roger/#_

It Looks Like This, **by Rafi Mittlefehldt. Candlewick Press, 2016. (G)**

Mike's father has transplanted the family to a new state, new schools, and a new evangelical church, despite Mike's protests. Furthermore, Dad is overly anxious to "toughen up" Mike by pushing him into sports and away from art. But Mike meets Sean, and their time together increases until they spend one unforgettable night at the beach. They are outed by camera-wielding bully Victor, and dire consequences ensue. Mike is sent to church conversion camp and Sean takes his life. Told in powerful prose, this haunting story will stay with readers long after they close the book.

Conversation Starters

1. What are conversion camps? Can LGBTQAI+ people be converted? Why or why not?
2. How do you feel about Mike's family, especially his father and sister?
3. Why did Victor behave the way he did? Does he take some responsibility for the consequences his actions have in Mike's and Sean's lives?

Resources

- Author's official website: www.rafimitt.com

The Last Exit to Normal, **by Michael Harmon. Knopf, 2008. (G)**

Ben Campbell is having a rotten time. His gay dads, who are not the problem, decide they all need a fresh start because Ben has been making some inappropriate choices. They decide to move to where his father Ed was born, Rough Butte, Montana. Ben has stereotypical thoughts of what this place will be like, and that doesn't change when he looks out the window of his new room at his new grandmother's house to see a dead deer hanging on the back porch of their nearest neighbor. While Ben is trying to put his life back together, he also tries to help his abused neighbor. This book has many layers to dig through while breaking through stereotypes. However, teens will be glad they took the time to read this funny, poignant book.

Awards and Honors

- Starred reviews: KLIATT, March 1, 2008; *Publishers Weekly*, February 18, 2008; *School Library Journal*, April 1, 2008

Conversation Starters

1. Did you have to move after you entered high school? What kinds of challenges did you face? How did you overcome them?
2. The overarching theme of this book is "You can't judge a book (town or parent) by its cover." In what ways does the protagonist of the book handle moving to a new town? How is he forced to change his preconceptions?

Last Seen Leaving, by Caleb Roehrig. Feiwel and Friends, 2016. (G)

This spine-chilling mystery centers around Flynn Doherty, whose girlfriend, January, is missing. He's questioned by police, while secretly recalling the last time he and his girlfriend were together. She pressed him for sex, he refused, and she declared him gay, a truth he'd yet to admit. While he's a suspect, Flynn sets out to solve her disappearance with his friend Kaz, with whom Flynn eventually develops a romantic relationship. They discover that January had quit her job, was behaving rather erratically, and was telling lies about Flynn. Even though the situations are somewhat sensationalized, the voice and struggles ring true. It's fast paced, with a twist of an ending.

Awards and Honors

- Starred reviews: *Booklist*, October 15, 2016; *Kirkus Reviews*, August 1, 2016; *Publishers Weekly*, October 24, 2016; *School Library Connection*, January 1, 2017

Conversation Starters

1. Why do you think January pressed Flynn to take the relationship to the next level? What do you think about Flynn's response?
2. What's the role of Kaz? For Flynn? In solving the mystery?
3. What do you think of the conclusion? How would you change it?

Resources

- Author's official website: http://calebroehrig.com

Luna: A Novel, by Julie Ann Peters. Little Brown, 2004 (T)

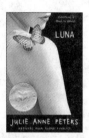

In one of the first published young adult books with a transgender character, we meet Liam and his sister, Regan. The reader learns both of their stories: First is the story of how Liam knows she is a girl in a boy's body, discovers a way to express herself as Luna, and, finally, begins to transition. The other story is Regan's. She loves her brother and has always realized that Liam is female on the inside. Regan does what she can to support and protect Liam by allowing Liam to enter her room at night and transform into Luna and by acting as a buffer between Luna and her parents. This, at times, causes her issues at school with both friends and boyfriends, but Regan remains true to Luna. Through this story told in both the present tense and through flashbacks, we learn the poignant passionate, occasionally rocky road to Luna's living as her true self.

Awards and Honors

- Starred reviews: *Kirkus Reviews*, April 1, 2004

Conversation Starters

1. Do you believe that all people have deep secrets or unexpressed thoughts they are carrying with them?
2. How do you think situations have changed for those who identify as transgender? Or haven't they?
3. What is your opinion of Regan and how she allowed Luna to change her life? Was it for the better? Why or why not?

The Miseducation of Cameron Post, by Emily M. Danforth. Balzer and Bray, 2012. (L)

Age twelve is a dramatic and traumatic year for Cameron. She kisses a girl for the first time, and her parents die in a car accident. At first, she feels guilt and believes the first has caused the second, but eventually she realizes the two are not connected. As a result of these events, she is sent to live in Montana with her religiously conservative aunt who requires her to attend church. Cameron begins to realize her lesbian feelings and acts out in ways that land her in trouble. This all comes to a critical point when she is caught kissing Coley at a church function. Coley, a closeted bisexual, blames the issue on Cameron, whose aunt sends her to God's Promise, a camp designed to "cure" one of homosexuality. There Cameron comes to realize there are others like herself, and she begins to make friends and knows she will be able to survive. A raw and dark story at so many points, it still reveals the hope and eventual power of allowing yourself to become who you are.

Awards and Honors

- Starred reviews: *Booklist*, December 15, 2011; *Kirkus Reviews*, December 15, 2011; *Publishers Weekly*, January 9, 2012; *School Library Journal*, March 1, 2012

Conversation Starters

1. Religion conversion camps still exist. Are they a viable choice? Why or why not?
2. Do you think sorrow and guilt over her parents' deaths caused Cameron to act the way she did?

Resources

- Author's official website: www.emdanforth.com

Openly Straight, by Bill Konigsberg. Arthur A. Levine Books, 2013. (G)

Rafe is a boy who is out, is accepted by his peers, and even speaks on the topic at other high schools. When he moves East to attend an all-boys boarding school, Rafe decides that he just wants to be known for himself, not as the gay student, so he decides to play it straight. This works temporarily, until Rafe falls for Ben. This is a smart, engaging, and entertaining book that makes readers think about truly being themselves.

Awards and Honors

- Starred reviews: *Booklist*, June 1, 2013; *Bulletin of the Center for Children's Books*, July 1, 2013; *Library Media Connection*, November 1, 2013

Conversation Starters

1. Have you ever wanted to move and start over as a new person?
2. How would you deal with a friend who confided to you that he or she is not who he or she seems to be?
3. How important is it to you to be your true self in front of others? How far would you go to make that happen?

Resources

- Author's official website: https://billkonigsberg.com

The Other F-Word, by Natasha Friend. Farrar Straus Giroux, 2017. (L)

What's the other f-word? Family, of course. In this part-drama, part-humor, part-mystery title, we meet Hollis, sperm donor daughter of two moms, who felt she needed to meet her half-sibling, Milo, when she was six. Now, ten years later, Milo reconnects with Hollis because of his life-threatening health issues, and he wants her to help her seek out their sperm donor dad. After some convincing, she relents and they go on a paper, and physical, chase to track him down. Throughout this journey, they discover three more half-siblings, two of whom join the chase. This fast-paced story flows with strong description and characterization and a fun sense of cageyness. There's absolutely nothing stereotypical about family in this story.

Awards and Honors

- Starred reviews: *Booklist*, January 1, 2017; *Publishers Weekly*, January 9, 2017

Conversation Starters

1. What role do the mothers, both of Hollis's and Milo's, play in creating this situation? What role do they play in the solution?
2. What do you see as beneficial in these siblings' relationships? Anything harmful?
3. Should there be a sequel? If so, suggest ideas for the plot.

Resources

- Author's official website: www.natashafriend.com

The Perks of Being a Wallflower, by Stephen Chbosky. MTV Books/ Pocket Books, 1999. (G)

As a young adult novel, this story does contain its fair share of teen angst, but it is so much more. Its themes include coming out, suicide, and teen pregnancy—a roller coaster of events that raise a variety of emotions for those reading it. The story is told through a series of letters that Charlie writes to a character the reader never meets. Using letters is a more intimate way to communicate everything Charlie goes through his freshman year of high school. Because many students are questioning at this age, this is a good book to recommend, as it allows readers to experience situations vicariously.

Awards and Honors

- YALSA's Best Books for Young Adults, 2000
- YALSA's Quick Picks for Reluctant Young Adult Readers, 2000

Conversation Starters

1. Why do you think this is, or isn't, a realistic portrayal of high school?
2. Who do you think is the recipient of Charlie's letters?
3. What would you say to Charlie in a letter? Or would you rather write a letter to another character? Who would that be?
4. What factors or elements in this story make it a successful movie? Which do you think is better, the book or the movie? Defend your answer.

Resources

- Pennsylvania Center for the Book's author biography: https://pabook.libraries.psu.edu/literary-cultural-heritage-map-pa/bios/Chbosky__Stephen

---

Rainbow Boys, by Alex Sanchez. Simon Pulse, 2001. (G)

In this first of several YA novels written by Alex Sanchez that deal with homosexuality in an open and honest way, we meet three high school seniors, Jason, Kyle, and Nelson. One is a jock who publicly has a girlfriend, one has not come out yet, and one is openly gay. The importance and appeal of this book is that it not only shows the emotional struggles that come with being a senior in high school but also showcases dealing with the added issues of being homosexual. In 2001, this book was challenged because of its honest and frank portrayal of homosexuality. However, the deftly and beautifully created characters share with us the true emotions of gay teens.

Awards and Honors

- Starred review: *Bulletin of the Center for Children's Books*, November 1, 2001

Conversation Starters

1. When you moved from middle to high school, did your circle of friends change? Do you know why?

2. They say everyone carries a secret. What do you think about that? Do you agree or not?
3. What would you say is the theme of this story?

Resources

- Author's official website: www.alexsanchez.com

Seven Ways We Lie, by Riley Redgate. Amulet Books, 2016. (B, A)

Told from seven different characters' points of view, with each character trying to resist one of the seven deadly sins, this story centers around an all-American girl, Juniper. She accidentally reveals that she's having a relationship with a faculty member. In attempting to keep this hidden, the other six characters are drawn into the collective plot, while also dealing with their own secrets and trying to save face.  They struggle with wrath, greed, sloth, pride, lust, envy, and gluttony as they support one another. There is a pansexual character and an asexual character, whose stories aren't so much about their sexuality, though that is an important part of their identities. The story moves quickly as the characters' foibles push the reader along.

Conversation Starters

1. What are the seven deadly sins? What is their origin?
2. Do they work successfully as a structure for this book?
3. How does each character's sexuality, or lack of it, drive the story forward?

Resources

- Author's official website: www.rileyredgate.com

True Letters from a Fictional Life, by Kenneth Logan. HarperTeen, 2016. (G)

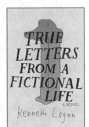

With both wit and intrigue, Logan relates the life of James, who on the surface is the "all American boy." But he has a secret side, he's a closeted gay, which he reveals only in letters to his somewhat girlfriend, other friends, and family members. But he never mails those letters, choosing to hide his story away in a drawer. However, the letters are stolen and mailed to their intended recipients just as James is beginning a relationship with Topher. There's nearly constant homophobia expressed by the book's characters, but that's not unrealistic in this upper-middle-class town in Vermont. Logan does manage to reconcile his two personas in a way that's satisfying to him.

Awards and Honors

- Starred review: *Kirkus Reviews*, April 1, 2016

Conversation Starters

1. Was writing a satisfactory way for Logan to deal with his anxiety? Do you write to make sense of your world? Is it helpful?
2. There's an abundance of homophobia in this book. Do you feel it's appropriate in this case? Why or why not?
3. This book is told in lighthearted terms but includes mystery and sorrow. Does it work in this case?

Resources

- Author's YouTube video: www.youtube.com/watch?v=cjAR0VPT6bw

Unbecoming, by Jenny Downham. David Fickling Books/Scholastic, 2016. (L)

Originally published in England, this timeless story of three generations of women is woven together by Katie, the youngest. At seventeen, Katie is struggling with her sexuality and the walkout of her father when her grandmother, Mary, an Alzheimer's patient becomes in need of a caregiver. Mary, a free-spirited character, with secrets in her past, upsets the delicate family balance. Katie's mother, Caroline, who is stressed by her single motherhood of Katie and her special-needs brother, wage earning, and now the care of her estranged mother, has secrets of her own. As Katie and Mary's relationship strengthens and the past is revealed, family bonds are stretched to the limit and then repaired.

Awards and Honors

- Starred reviews: *Horn Book*, January 1, 2016; *Horn Book Guide*, October 1, 2016; *Kirkus Reviews*, November 15, 2015; *Publishers Weekly*, November 23, 2015; *School Library Journal*, December 1, 2015
- Stonewall Honor Book, 2017

Conversation Starters

1. Have you had a special relationship with an older person? Why do you think your bonds were close?
2. What is there about Katie and Mary's relationship that lets Mary relive her life before she dies? And that lets Katie understand and express her true self?
3. Is Caroline justified in her feelings toward both Katie and Mary? What kinds of pressures do parents with many family obligations feel?

Resources

- Book review webpage: www.teenreads.com/reviews/unbecoming-0

The Upside of Unrequited, by Becky Albertalli. Balzar and Bray, 2017. (L, B)

Twins Molly and Cassie have always been close, but Cassie has a new girlfriend, Mina, a pansexual Korean American, and she seems to be pulling away from Molly, who's been through twenty-six crushes but has had no boyfriends. Then, into Molly's life walk two boys, Mina's good friend Will and coworker Reid. Molly is heavy, has no problem with it, but feels that others do, despite what her mothers tell

her. The story weaves through Molly's negotiating a new relationship with her sister, falling for Reid and his requited affection, participating in her mothers' wedding, and gaining a new understanding of herself. Written in strong voices, clipped dialogue, and a breezy pace, this a fun, satisfying read.

Awards and Honors

- Starred reviews: *School Library Journal*, February 1, 2017; *VOYA* (*Voice of Youth Advocates*), April 1, 2017

Conversation Starters

1. How does Molly's relationship with Cassie change? Does sexuality play a role?
2. How does Molly's physical appearance play into her story?
3. What is the role of the family? Of her baby brother and two mothers? What kind of support do they offer?

Resources

- Author's official website: www.beckyalbertalli.com

We Are the Ants, by Shaun David Hutchinson. Simon Pulse, 2016. (G)

Is the world worth saving? Harry Denton has 144 days to decide, according to his alien captors. But is the world, and his life, really worth saving? His family is barely staying afloat, financially and emotionally, and his boyfriend betrayed him by committing suicide the year before. He's tormented at school, has a continuous one-night stand with the school's biggest bully, and dreads waking up each day. But then Diego arrives, the brilliant and mysterious new boy in school who helps Harry see life, and the world, in a whole different light. The reader will cheer for Harry, all the while wondering if his captors are real or a metaphor for his angst or both? This story is beautifully written and contains gems of wisdom.

Awards and Honors

- Starred reviews: *Booklist*, October 1, 2015; *Kirkus Reviews*, October 1, 2015; *Publishers Weekly*, December 14, 2015; *School Library Connection*, April 1, 2016; *School Library Journal*, November 1, 2015

Conversation Starters

1. If Diego hadn't come into Harry's life, would it be worth living? Why or why not?
2. What words of Diego's do you find inspiring?
3. What would you do if you could choose to end the world? Why?
4. Are the aliens real or metaphorical? Defend your answer.

Resources

- Author's official website: http://shaundavidhutchinson.com

Weetzie Bat, by Francesca Lia Block. Harper and Row, 1989. (G)

This book shattered concepts of what a young adult title could be. The author called it an urban fairy tale, with its fantastical fantasized view of Los Angeles, or Shangri-L.A., as it is called in the book. We meet Weetzie Bat in high school; she is described as a skinny, unusual girl with a bleach-blonde flat-top haircut, a love of Indian culture, and a quirky sense of style. Her best friend is Dirk, who has blue eyes and a black Mohawk. After a while as friends, he comes out to her, which she views as no big deal. In fact, that is the joy and whimsy of this story: they are confronted with life—dysfunctional families, unconventional friends, AIDS, death—and yet for the most part, Weetzie and Dirk take these things in stride, almost marginalizing them, which may be one of the reasons this book was so popular; those students who felt disenfranchised or marginalized could read the story and realize that issues are only as big as you make them, and being true to yourself is the most important thing. There are a few magical incidents in the story, hence, the fairy tale descriptor. For example, Dirk's grandmother gives Weetzie a gold object that contains a genie who gives her three wishes. The magic is not germane to the story; it is the results of the wishes and how they impact

Weetzie's life plan that are telling. The book was often censored because of topics such as out-of-wedlock sex and gay sex (although both of these are more implied than detailed), rape, drugs, and other adult situations, but these are not major events in the story, just incidents that the characters use to grow into stronger people. This was the first of seven books about the characters. They definitely served an important purpose, as many adults talk about the power and impact the books had on their teen years.

Awards and Honors

- Association for Library Service to Children's Notable Children's Book, 1995
- Children's Literature Association's Phoenix Award, 2009

Conversation Starters

1. One thing absent in this story is prejudices. What kind of response do you think these characters would face today?
2. Introducing a genie granting wishes put a real spin on the story. How do you think Weetzie Bat's and Dirk's lives would have progressed without that intervention?
3. Do any of the characters in this book remind you of someone you know? Why or why not?
4. Which character would you like to sit down and have coffee with? What would you like to talk about?

Resources

- Author's official website: http://francescaliablock.com

***

Will Grayson, Will Grayson, by David Levithan and John Green. Dutton Juvenile, 2010. (G)

What happens when two Will Graysons meet at a porn shop in Chicago? A lot. One is gay, the other straight; and their lives become intertwined. There is love and loss, theater, and a huge friend named Tiny, all of which combine to make this a positive story for all teens, not just those who are part of the LGBTQAI+ community.

Awards and Honors

- Stonewall Book Award, 2011

Conversation Starters

1. Which Will Grayson do you identify with? Why?
2. Do you have a friend who is a total opposite of you? What attracted you to that person?
3. What do you think this book is really about?

Resources

- Authors' official webpages: www.johngreenbooks.com/will-grayson -will-grayson and www.davidlevithan.com/will-grayson-will-grayson

---

You Know Me Well, by Nina LaCour and David Levithan. St. Martin's Griffin, 2016. (L, G)

Set in San Francisco during Pride Week, this story relates how classmates Mark and Kate discover each other and quickly cement a friendship. What do they have in common? They are both gay, and they quickly become cheerleaders for each other. Mark convinces crush Ryan, a closeted gay, to attend the festivities, but Ryan falls for another guy. Kate has a meeting place set up with her crush, Violet, but then Kate backs out. What ensues is a week-long romp between friends that leaves them both wiser for it in the joyful, yet not perfect ending. Writing in chapters that alternate between the two characters, LaCour and Levithan employ prose and dialogue in strong, genuine voices.

Conversation Starters

1. Are Kate and Mark true friends? How do you know?
2. How meaningful is their friendship to both of them?
3. The authors write this book in alternating voices. Is this technique effective? How is each character developed in this way?
4. What is your opinion of the ending? Would you change it? If so, how?

Resources

- Authors' official websites: www.davidlevithan.com and http://nina lacour.com/home

FANTASY

When the Moon Was Ours, by Anna-Marie McLemore. Thomas Dunne Books, 2016. (L, T)

They say Miel came from an old water tower, when it tipped over in the village. They say Sam is a strange boy who paints the moon and stars wherever he goes. But regardless, the two develop a close relationship, as it seems no one else understands them. As Miel matures, roses begin to grow out of her arms, and they are coveted by the four vixen Bonner sisters. They believe that the roses can make anyone fall in love with them. To obtain the roses, they torment Miel and threaten to reveal Sam for his true biological self. Through it all, the relationship of Miel and Sam survives.

Awards and Honors

- Starred reviews: *Booklist*, September 15, 2016; *Kirkus Reviews*, August 1, 2016; *Publishers Weekly*, March 7, 2016; *School Library Journal*, August 1, 2016; *VOYA* (*Voice of Youth Advocates*), June 1, 2016
- Stonewall Honor Book, 2017
- National Book Awards Longlist, Young People's Literature, 2016

Conversation Starters

1. Can you buy into Miel and Sam's story? Why or why not?
2. Are the Bonner sisters protagonists or antagonists? Defend your answer.
3. What do you think about Sam's role as a boy in his family, in the absence of a father? How does he feel about it?

Resources

- Author's official website: http://author.annamariemclemore.com

INFORMATIONAL BOOKS

Beyond Magenta: Transgender Teens Speak Out, **by Susan Kuklin.
Candlewick Press, 2014. (T, A, I)**

This is a gritty, no-holds-barred series of interviews with six teens who are transgender, intersex, and/or asexual. These unique testaments by youth cover a variety of home arrangements, family support systems, childhood experiences, and bullying situations. The teens are honest and open in relating their stories about life, love, and identity. Kuklin comments on the teens' stories and has included touching photographs in a way that allows the teens to show who they truly are in their own ways.

Awards and Honors

- Starred reviews: *Booklist*, February 1, 2014; *Bulletin of the Center for Children's Books*, February 1, 2014; *Kirkus Reviews*, December 15, 2013; *Publishers Weekly*, November 18, 2013; *VOYA* (*Voice of Youth Advocates*), April 1, 2014
- Stonewall Honor Book, 2015

Conversation Starters

1. Do you see these six teens as brave? Why or why not? If so, in what ways?
2. Are you willing to tell your story, at least to yourself? If so, what avenue would you choose to do so?
3. What do you hope for next in these teens' lives? In your life?

Resources

- Author-photographer's official website: www.susankuklin.net

***In Real Life: My Journey to a Pixelated World,* by Joey Graceffa.
Keywords Press, 2015. (G)**

In an engaging storyteller's voice that teens will immediately identify from his YouTube videos, Graceffa tells his life story . . . so far. As a young adult, with a very strong YouTube audience, he reaches back into his childhood to relate the stories of his family's breakup due to his mother's alcoholism, his sister's both rivalry and fierce protection, his father's connection from afar, his stepfather's support, and welcoming his autistic brother. He tells of the bullying he received in school, his struggle to be both himself and accepted by others, his attempt at college, the beginnings of his career, and his coming out to both himself and others. Each breezy chapter is followed by words of wisdom, lists of resources, and bits of humor and advice.

Conversation Starters

1. Does Joey's voice sound genuine to you? Give examples to support your answer.
2. How do you feel about his family members? Who gave the most support and why?
3. What's your favorite advice that Joey offers? Will you take it?

Resources

- Author's official YouTube channel: www.youtube.com/user/JoeyGraceffa/featured
- Author's official website: http://joeygraceffa.com

Additional Biographies by YouTubers

- *Buffering: Unshared Tales of a Life Fully Loaded,* by Hannah Hart (Dey St., 2016; L)
- *Binge,* by Tyler Oakley (Simon and Schuster, 2015; G)

LGBTQ+ Athletes Claim the Field: Striving for Equality, by Kirstin Cronn-Mills. Twenty-First Century Books, 2017. (L, G, B, T, Q)

This solid, attractive book is a look at the history of trans people in sports and how difficult it is for them to be part of a team. Cronn-Mills writes in a very matter-of-fact tone, heartfelt but not emotional, using a myriad of examples. She includes many well-reproduced photos and several extra features: timeline, source notes, glossary, bibliography, index, and photo credits. One exceptional feature at the beginning of the book is an introduction by Alex Jackson Nelson, a trans man athlete, who frames Cronn-Mills's book with his experience in team sports and the continuing fight for equality.

Awards and Honors

- Starred review: *Booklist*, September 1, 2016

Conversation Starters

1. Read the questions posed by Nelson on page 6 of the introduction. Why does he include these for LGBTQ+ athletes? Are they critical? Are there more you would add?
2. What is your experience with team sports?
3. How can you join the fight for equality for LGBTQ+ athletes in the world of sports?

Resources

- Author's official website: http://kirstincronn-mills.com
- Blog post interview with both Cronn-Mills and Nelson: https://lernerbooks.blog/2017/03/meet-kirstin-cronn-mills-and-alex-jackson-nelson.html

Queer, There, and Everywhere: 23 People Who Changed the World, by
Sarah Prager. Harper, 2017. (L, G, B, T, Q, A, I)

In this rockin' collective biography, Prager selects some
well-known, and some not as well-known, individuals
who pushed the boundaries of gender and sexuality.
From an introduction that in a spirited voice gives the
background on gender/sexual diversity worldwide to
the scandalous teenage Roman emperor Elagabalus, to
Abraham Lincoln, to present-day actor George Takei, to
the abundance of back matter, this highly researched
work was very difficult to put down. Each bold story is
told with respect and dignity, pointing out the person's unique contribution
to gender/sexual diversity. An endnote looks to the future and is followed
by a very helpful glossary and a bibliography with source notes that authen-
ticates this highly engaging book.

Awards and Honors

- Starred reviews: *Kirkus Reviews*, March 15, 2017; *Publishers Weekly*,
  May 15, 2017

Conversation Starters

1. How many of these historical figures are you familiar with? How many
   are new to you?
2. Did you know their stances against the heteronormative culture in
   which they lived? Are you surprised by any of their lives?
3. Do you identify with any of their stories? What can you learn from
   them?
4. If you could share only one of these stories with your family or friends,
   which one would it be? Why?

Resources

- Author's official website: http://sarahprager.com

PROGRAM/THEME/DISPLAY IDEAS

Young people in this age group are a mix of contradictions. They want to conform with everything trending and yet be individuals. They wish to be considered as adults, while still having someone else take responsibility for their actions. They are at varying levels of self-awareness. All of this can make creating events and programming for teens challenging; you never know who might attend and how the teens see themselves. So why not try something open-ended, something similar to an unconference—a "Talkathon"? Set up a space/place, a date, and a schedule of ten- to fifteen-minute time increments, and then invite teens to register. Explain there is not a set theme, that this is just a way for them to talk to others who share an interest or passion. Mention that they might get the chance to connect with someone who understands what they are feeling. The idea is to foster communication and the opportunity for a day of sharing geared toward teens.

Survey teens visiting your library about their interests, and challenge them to take charge of a time slot to discuss that topic. If your space allows, you could hold several talks simultaneously with small-group spaces for five or fewer and a large space for a bigger crowd. This event could be marketed in many ways. A teen advisory board, if you have one, could take charge of advertising, which might include posters, both print and electronic, and social media, like Twitter and Instagram, in addition to traditional marketing. Create a brainstormed list of ideas to get your teens thinking:

Have you ever considered . . .
I was thinking about . . .
Does anyone else like . . .
My favorite thing is . . .
Let me tell you my point of view . . .
I don't like it when . . .
I would like to see . . .
I would like to learn more about . . .
Could we try . . .
Could we create . . .
What would happen if . . .

Then challenge leaders to sign up or to suggest other people they could ask to take charge. The talk spaces would not need facilitators, just group members willing to listen. Ideally, these "talks" would lead to positive connections and possibly the formation of new interest groups. Since your goal is to build support systems for teens who are gay, trans, and/or questioning, you will want to provide the opportunity for some talks about these topics. A local organization might have someone interested in registering for a block of time. For example, a local organization, Kaleidoscope, near our school district, provides spaces and education for LGBTQAI+ teens. Check Stonewall groups or the Trevor Project online to find groups in your area.

CONCLUSION

The teen years can be the most turbulent of times, and yet they can be the most joyful as well. These years are a time of continued identity searching and new relationships developing, some friendly, others romantic. Teens are looking beyond family to future plans and becoming independent adults. But at the same time, teens are insecure, vulnerable, and often immature. Guidance is still necessary, and books are one of the best venues for adolescents to try on different personas to see how they feel. We must make these books available for all young adults, those who are searching as well as those who just like to read good books. Whatever their purpose for reading, interacting with books with LGBTQAI+ characters or themes allows a young person to learn that similarities and differences make the world a better place.

The books listed in this chapter are a mixture of newer and classic titles, but they represent some of the best in LGBTQAI+ titles for all teens. These books are mature—some are quite edgy—but they are high-quality works that will engage teens. They should be an easy sell through your recommendations or a display. And never underestimate the power teens have for influencing one another. Possibly invite teens to add to a display area the authors and titles of books they've enjoyed and would recommend.

As with the titles chosen for younger and middle grade readers, the books listed in this chapter need be available to all children. They validate emotions, actions, and thoughts while simultaneously encouraging understanding and compassion for others.

"I am both happy and sad at the same time, and I'm still trying to figure out how that could be."[2]

–STEPHEN CHBOSKY, *THE PERKS OF BEING A WALLFLOWER*

NOTES

1. Nick Duerden, "David Levithan Interview: The US Author on Leading the Way in LGBT Fiction for Young Adults," *The Independent*, March 16, 2015, www.independent.co.uk/arts-entertainment/books/features/david-levithan-interview-the-us-author-on-leading-the-way-in-lgbt-fiction-for-young-adults-10112154.html.

2. "Quote by Stephen Chbosky," Quotery.com, accessed July 23, 2017, www.quotery.com/quotes/i-am-both-happy-and-sad-at-the-same-time.

BIBLIOGRAPHY

Albertalli, Becky. *The Upside of Unrequited.* New York: Balzar and Bray, 2017.

Beam, Cris. *I Am J.* New York: Little, Brown, 2011.

Block, Francesca Lia. *Weetzie Bat.* HarperCollins, 1989.

Brown, Jaye Robin. *Georgia Peaches and Other Forbidden Fruit.* New York: HarperTeen, 2016.

Charlton-Trujillo, e. E. *Fat Angie.* Somerville, MA: Candlewick Press, 2013.

Chbosky, Stephen. *The Perks of Being a Wallflower.* New York: MTV Books/Pocket Books, 1999.

Cronn-Mills, Kirstin. *LGBTQ+ Athletes Claim the Field: Striving for Equality.* Minneapolis, MN: Twenty-First Century Books, 2017.

Danforth, Emily M. *The Miseducation of Cameron Post.* New York: Balzer and Bray, 2012.

Downham, Jenny. *Unbecoming.* New York: David Fickling Books/Scholastic, 2016.

Federle, Tim. *The Great American Whatever.* New York: Simon and Schuster, 2016.

Friend, Natasha. *The Other F-Word.* New York: Farrar Straus Giroux, 2017.

Garden, Nancy. *Annie on My Mind.* New York: Farrar Straus Giroux, 1982.

George, Madeleine. *The Difference between You and Me.* New York: Viking Children's Books, 2012.

Graceffa, Joey. *In Real Life: My Journey to a Pixelated World.* New York: Keywords Press, 2015.

Harmon, Michael. *The Last Exit to Normal.* New York: Knopf, 2008.

Hart, Hannah. *Buffering: Unshared Tales of a Life Fully Loaded*. New York: Dey St., 2016.

Hutchinson, Shaun David. *We Are the Ants*. New York: Simon Pulse, 2016.

Katcher, Brian. *Almost Perfect*. New York: Ember, 2009.

Koerge, Ron. *Arizona Kid*. Joy Street Books/Little Brown, 1988.

Konigsberg, Bill. *Openly Straight*. New York: Arthur A. Levine Books, 2013.

Kuklin, Susan. *Beyond Magenta: Transgender Teens Speak Out*. Somerville, MA: Candlewick Press, 2014.

LaCour, Nina, and David Levithan. *You Know Me Well*. New York: St. Martin's Griffin, 2016.

Levithan, David. *Boy Meets Boy*. New York: Alfred A. Knopf, 2003.

Levithan, David, and John Green. *Will Grayson, Will Grayson*. Dutton Juvenile, 2010.

Logan, Kenneth. *True Letters from a Fictional Life*. New York: HarperTeen, 2016.

McLemore, Anna-Marie. *When the Moon Was Ours*. New York: Thomas Dunne Books, 2016.

Mittlefehldt, Rafi. *It Looks Like This*. Somerville, MA: Candlewick Press, 2016.

Oakley, Tyler. *Binge*. New York: Simon and Schuster, 2015.

Peters, Julie Ann. *Luna: A Novel*. New York: Little Brown, 2004.

Prager, Sarah. *Queer, There, and Everywhere: 23 People Who Changed the World*. Illustrated by Zoe More O'Farrell. New York: Harper, 2017.

Redgate, Riley. *Seven Ways We Lie*. New York: Amulet Books, 2016.

Roehrig, Caleb. *Last Seen Leaving*. New York: Feiwel and Friends, 2016.

Russo, Meredith. *If I Was Your Girl*. New York: Flatiron Books, 2016.

Saenz, Benjamin Alire. *The Inexplicable Logic of My Life*. New York: Clarion Books, 2017.

Sanchez, Alex. *Rainbow Boys*. New York: Simon Pulse, 2001.

Silvera, Adam. *History Is All You Left Me*. New York: Soho Teen, 2017.

Whaley, John Corey. *Highly Illogical Behavior*. New York: Dial Books, 2016.

Wittinger, Ellen. *Hard Love*. New York: Simon and Schuster, 1999.

It's about Basic Human Rights

Open, honest talk is needed whenever a child realizes and/or questions his or her gender and sexuality. Chapters 1 through 3 have been our way of giving you, the reader and practitioner, several tools to work with:

1. Lists and annotations of quality LGBTQAI+ children's and young adult literature, both new and classic
2. Conversation-starting questions that will hopefully get children thinking and talking both about themselves and others
3. Resources that you can pull additional information from to enhance the books
4. Theme ideas that are developmentally appropriate for the age level and that can be adapted for school libraries, public libraries, and classrooms
5. Reasons for using these books with all children/young adults, while offering guidelines for working with other stakeholders

And as we argue, it's never too early to begin the conversations. As children's/young adult librarians and teachers, you owe it to your patrons to have the very best possible books ready and available to them at their point of need. Sadly, this does not always happen, for a variety of reasons, including self-censorship. Oftentimes, librarians may not even be aware that this is what they are practicing. We often hear comments like the following when talking with school librarians about LGBTQAI+ books:

"I have such a small budget that if there is a chance of being challenged, I will move on to other items to purchase."

"There are too many other options out there for me to choose from."

"My community is just too conservative to waste my money on books that
    won't circulate."
These quotations were gleaned from a survey Liz administered before
presenting a session on banned books.[1] This way of thinking, whether it be
censorship by self-selection or rigid thinking in collection curation, deprives
patrons of the right books at the right time.

In some cases, school librarians have justified not purchasing LGBTQAI+
books because they say students are not asking for them. Indeed, in settings
with this sort of "Don't ask, don't tell" attitude, questioning students might
feel vulnerable and at risk were they to request such titles.

As has been discussed, the library can, and should be, the safe haven
for all students, whatever their beliefs or gender identification. How many
LGBTQAI+ students say that reading about others like themselves makes
them feel validated? These students deserve representation in the school
library collection as much as any other group does. We, as professionals,
have done this for other sensitive topics, and this one is just as personal
and important—possibly more so.

Adults, both we as practitioners and other stakeholders, need to realize
and affirm that it's a matter of basic human rights afforded to all. Whatever
our beliefs, values, religions, political stances, we aren't the important piece
of the equation—the child is. We need to step back, evaluate the child's
needs, and provide the resources and opportunities to allow the child to
learn, question, and grow while encouraging others outside the LGBTQAI+
community to understand and develop empathy. To do this, we need to not
only purchase materials but also make sure those materials are visible to
students. When teachers ask for book lists or librarians give book talks,
make sure these books are included.

A study conducted by University of Central Arkansas's Assistant Pro-
fessor Wendy Rickman, involving LGBTQAI+ resources in school libraries
in Arkansas prior to 2015, concluded most participants:

- have LGBTQAI+ fiction titles on the shelves;
- have no nonfiction LGBTQAI+ titles or other resources;
- have not utilized the ALA Stonewall Book Awards and Rainbow Lists
  from which to select book titles;
- had no professional development about serving LGBTQAI+ patrons;
- responded negatively to having self-identified LGBTQAI+ patrons;

- responded positively to having patrons who have not yet identified as LGBTQAI+;
- had not seen or heard bullying tactics toward LGBTQAI+ students; and
- were reluctant to purchase LGBTQAI+ materials, and a few had been harassed for it.[2]

Rickman expressed a significant correlation between respondents who had received professional development and the willingness to provide LGBTQAI+ materials. If this study were to be repeated today and expanded to the country as a whole, we wonder how much progress has been made. This book is an attempt to help further this progress.

One example of a greater understanding of the changing nature of LGBTQAI+ is the recurrence of the phrase "two-spirited." This term "refers to a person who has both a masculine and a feminine spirit, and is used by some First Nations people to describe their sexual, gender and/or spiritual identity."[3] Originally, all First Nation societies acknowledged that there were three to five gender roles, and all were acceptable. When the early explorers came, they sought to do away with this multiple-genders belief. At the Third Annual Inter-tribal Native American, First Nations, Gay and Lesbian American Conference, held in Winnipeg in 1990, it was once again decided that a common term was needed, and two-spirited was selected. Different from bisexual, it is a more fluid term, one that is gaining popularity. Books with two-spirited characters are needed and are one example of how children's and young adult literature should evolve to respond to the LGBTQAI+ community.

It's now our hope that you take the tools we've offered and put them to work in your community and situation with your unique population. Debra L. Whelan, in her article "Out and Ignored," offers some suggestions for all librarians wanting to create a more welcoming environment for LGBTQAI+ groups:

- Make sure your collection development and challenge policies are clear and that staff understand the procedure.
- Clarify your library's equal opportunity statement so that it includes the terms "gender and sexual orientation."
- Have positive reviews that support your materials.
- Protect workplace speech.

- Conduct staff training to guard against misperceptions and prejudice.
- Create/maintain a Teen Advisory Board.
- Network with local GSA (Gay-Straight Alliance) and other LGBTQAI+ groups for support and education.
- Make materials available and accessible through book talks, displays, and more.[4]

Throughout the course of researching and writing this book, parts of the political and social landscape in the United States have turned from intolerant to hostile toward all diverse communities, including LGBTQAI+ individuals. Volatile rhetoric, acts of violence, legislation, and more have fanned the flames of fear, intolerance, and hate. Yet, on the other side, marches, demonstrations, social media campaigns, phone calls, and professional media coverage have increased to levels not seen since the 1960s. The danger is real and present, but the movement against the backward slide to closed-mindedness is being attacked in many ways. So we leave you with these thoughts:

- Allow your larger community to learn about the LGBTQAI+ community.
- Afford them opportunities to realize these are also people with regular jobs, families, and lives.
- Our commonalities far outweigh our differences.
- Finally, education is a very powerful tool. Use it to open the doors to understanding.

Hopefully, we are contributing to the push forward for diversity through this book. It is our hope that you can use the information we provide to improve access to, and motivation for reading, LGBTQAI+ literature for all children in your school library, public library, classroom, or wherever you teach and provide services to young people.

NOTES

1. Liz Deskins and Jody Casella, "Stacking the Shelf with 'Banned' Books" (address, AASL National Conference, Columbus Convention Center, Columbus, OH, November 7, 2015).

2. Wendy Rickman, "2.5 Million Teens," *Knowledge Quest* 43, no. 5 (2015): 22–27.

3. Peter H. Fewster, "Two-Spirit Community," Researching for LGBTQ Health, accessed July 25, 2017, http://lgbtqhealth.ca/community/two-spirit.php.

4. Debra Lau Whelan, "Out and Ignored: Why Are So Many School Libraries Reluctant to Embrace Gay Teens?" *School Library Journal* 52, no. 1 (2006): 46–50.

Appendix

Additional Resources

Organizations

GLSEN (Gay, Lesbian and Straight Education Network). www.glsen.org.

GLSEN is the leading national education organization focused on ensuring safe schools for all students. Established nationally in 1995, GLSEN envisions a world in which every child learns to respect and accept all people, regardless of sexual orientation or gender identity/expression. GLSEN seeks to develop school climates where difference is valued for the positive contribution it makes to creating a more vibrant and diverse community.

Human Rights Campaign (HRC). www.hrc.org.

The largest civil rights organization dedicated to equality for the LGBTQAI+ community, "HRC envisions a world where lesbian, gay, bisexual, transgender and queer people are embraced as full members of society at home, at work and in every community."

It Gets Better Project. www.itgetsbetter.org.

This organization's website features individuals, famous and not, telling their own personal LGBTQAI+ stories to show viewers they aren't alone. The organization allows anyone to submit their own stories and offers a list of phone numbers to call for help.

Lambda Legal. www.lambdalegal.org.

Lambda Legal is the foremost organization that offers legal advice to members of the LGBTQAI+ community. The website offers a state-by-state list of resources as well as several phone numbers.

Rainbow Book List—GLBTQ Books for Children and Teens. http://glbtrt.ala.org/ rainbowbooks.

This list is created by the Rainbow Book List Committee of the Gay, Lesbian, Bisexual, and Transgender Round Table of the American Library Association. This group presents an annual bibliography of quality books with significant and authentic GLBTQ content that are recommended for youth from birth through eighteen years old. Visitors to the site can click on "Suggestions" to recommend titles.

Southern Poverty Law Center (SPLC). www.splcenter.org.

The SPLC fights not only for LGBTQAI+ rights but for all marginalized groups who are discriminated against. The center retains a bank of lawyers who work to change laws, and the website keeps an up-to-date list of hate groups to watch out for.

Trevor Project. www.thetrevorproject.org.

This well-known national organization was founded in 1998 in response to the Academy Award–winning short film *Trevor*. It provides crisis and suicide prevention services to LGBTQ youth, aged thirteen through twenty-four. It also offers education programs and resources.

Articles

Alexander, Linda B. "Barriers to GLBTQ Collection Development and Strategies for Overcoming Them." *Young Adult Library Services* 5, no. 3 (2007): 43–49.

This article shares the research done that demonstrates that LGBTQAI+ teens are an underserved population in US libraries. It shows that both materials and programming are inadequate.

Barack, Lauren. "LGBTQ and You: How to Support Your Students." *School Library Journal* 60, no. 5 (2014): 40. www.slj.com/2014/05/diversity/lgbtq-you-how -to-support-your-students.

School libraries have many ways to support the LGBTQAI+ students they serve: using displays, book selection, and creating an unofficial refuge for teens who may not feel they have a place to be in school. This includes thoughtful book positioning for easy student access, whether the materials are "officially" checked out or not.

Chuang, Laura, George Raine, Denise Scott, and Kiera Tauro. "Out in Society, Invisible on the Shelves: Discussing LIS Literature about LGBTQ Youth." *Feliciter* 59, no. 5 (2013): 26–27.

The authors discuss the lack of evaluation of LGBTQAI+-related literature in the schools of library and information science. They also recommend including these titles in book talks and book clubs.

Hughes-Hassell, Sandra, Elizabeth Overberg, and Shannon Harris. "Lesbian, Gay, Bisexual, Transgender, and Questioning (LGBTQ)–Themed Literature for Teens: Are School Libraries Providing Adequate Collections?" *School Library Research* 16 (2013): 1–18. www.ala.org/aasl/slr/volume16/hughes-hassell-overberg-harris.

This article explains the results of a school library study of LGBTQAI+ books in collections. It showed that the number and variety of these books were inadequate but did not have a clear explanation of why. LGBTQAI+ teenagers feel marginalized in high school, often facing abuse and discrimination daily. The school librarian is in a position to provide even more than a safe haven for these teens by curating a collection that shares "positive, realistic images of the LGBTQ community." This study suggests that many school librarians are not doing so.

Lifshitz, Jessica. "Curating Empathy." *Literacy Today (2411–7862)* 33, no. 6 (2016): 24–26.

This article attempts to explain the importance of all libraries having a balanced collection, including classroom libraries. The author, an elementary school teacher speaks about wanting all of her students to be able to find themselves, their families, and their friends represented in the books on the shelves.

Naidoo, Jamie Campbell. "Over the Rainbow and Under the Radar." *Children and Libraries: The Journal of the Association for Library Service to Children* 11, no. 3 (2013): 34–40. Academic Search Premier, EBSCOhost (accessed July 28, 2017).

This article discusses the library services and programs offered for LGBTQ parents and their children. It also outlines the results of a research study funded by the ALA's Office of Diversity that evaluates the services of public libraries for the LGBTQ community in the United States.

Naidoo, Jamie Campbell, and Megan Roberts. "Serving ALL Families in Your Library: Inclusive Library Collections and Programs for LGBTQ Families and Children." Chicago: Association for Library Service to Children, 2016. www.ala.org/alsc/sites/ala.org.alsc/files/content/2016Institute/Serving%20ALL%20 Families%20in%20Your%20Library%20Inclusive%20Library%20Collections%20 and%20Programs%20for%20LGBTQ%20Families%20%26%20Children.pdf

This excellent list would be a great starting tool for creating a curated collection for LGBTQ families.

Parks, Alexander F. "Opening the Gate." *Young Adult Library Services* 10, no. 4 (2012): 22–27.

This article talks about using LGBTQAI+ literature in book talk programs to help teens deal with bullying and overcome homophobia. Lists of awards and websites are shared.

Pierce, Candi Garry. "Selection or Censorship? School Librarians and LGBTQ Resources." *School Libraries Worldwide* 21, no. 1 (2015): 73–90.

All students should have ready access to quality books of all kinds, including LGBTQAI+ resources. This study looked at possible variables to explain the reason some school library collections have a good representation of titles while others do not. One discovery was that school librarians practice self-censorship in building their collections. This study did demonstrate that licensed school librarians tend to have a more balanced collection.

Tadayuki, Suzuki, and Barbara Fiehn. "Taking a Closer Look." *Children and Libraries: The Journal of the Association for Library Service to Children* 14, no. 1 (2016): 14–19.

This article discusses the issue of a lack of LGBTQAI+ characters in books for intermediate-grade children. It discloses the lack of coverage in reviews and cataloging.

Whelan, Debra Lau. "Out and Ignored: Why Are so Many School Libraries Reluctant to Embrace Gay Teens?" *School Library Journal* 52, no. 1 (2006): 46–50.

This is a response to the 2003 National School Climate Survey, a biannual study by GLSEN. According to this article, only 50 percent of students say they have access to gay-related resources in their school media centers. The author puts forth the idea that librarians do not want to incite conflict and offers ways to build collections without book challenges.

Books

Abate, Michelle Ann, and Kenneth B. Kidd. *Over the Rainbow: Queer Children's and Young Adult Literature.* Ann Arbor, MI: University of Michigan, 2011.

This book is a collection of essays dedicated to LGBTQAI+ issues in children's and young adult literature. It was created to serve as both a scholarly work and a possible textbook.

Bausum, Ann. *Stonewall: Breaking Out in the Fight for Gay Rights.* New York: Viking, 2015.

This book covers the history of the turning point in the gay rights movement and its aftermath.

Cart, Michael, and Christine A. Jenkins. *Top 250 LGBTQ Books for Teens: Coming Out, Being Out, and the Search for Community.* Chicago: Huron Street Press, 2015.

This book offers an extensive annotated list of teen literature, both newer and classic, as well as professional resources.

Day, Frances Ann. *Lesbian and Gay Voices: An Annotated Bibliography and Guide to Literature for Children and Young Adults.* Westport, CT: Greenwood Press, 2000. Though now somewhat dated, this annotated bibliography includes picture books through young adult books in several genres.

Hillias, J. Martin, Jr., and James R. Murdock. *Serving Lesbian, Gay, Bisexual, Transgender, and Questioning Teens: A How-To-Do-It Manual for Librarians.* New York: Neal-Schuman, 2007.

This professional book includes collection development details, annotated book suggestions, and program ideas.

Mardell, Ashley. *The ABC's of LGBT+.* Coral Gables, FL: Mango Media, 2016.

Beginning with an extensive glossary, then using the alphabet as a framework to explore gender and sexuality, this handbook mixes information with anecdotes to add to the movement toward understanding and respect.

Naidoo, Jamie Campbell. *Rainbow Family Collections: Selecting and Using Children's Books with Lesbian, Gay, Bisexual, Transgender, and Queer Content.* Santa Barbara, CA: Libraries Unlimited, 2012.

This book provides an excellent list of books with LGBTQAI+ content and gives a synopsis of the books' contents. It concentrates more on children's books, an area often overlooked in research and book lists. It also discusses the history of LGBTQAI+ literature and awards and ways to present these books.

Savage, Dan, and Terry Miller, eds. *It Gets Better: Coming Out, Overcoming Bullying, and Creating a Life Worth Living.* New York: Penguin Group, 2012.

This collection of essays by famous, and not so famous, individuals is written for a young adult audience. The authors relate their experiences and assure readers that the future will be more positive.

Webber, Carlisle K. *Gay. Lesbian, Bisexual, Transgender and Questioning Teen Literature: A Guide to Reading Interests.* Santa Barbara, CA: Libraries Unlimited, 2010. This is an annotated list of young adult literature by genre and topic.

Blogs and Blog Posts

Adams, Helen. "June Is GLBT Book Month." *Knowledge Quest* (blog), June 1, 2017. http://knowledgequest.aasl.org/june-glbt-book-month.

This blog from the American Association of School Librarians addresses many areas of school librarianship. This June 2017 post is dedicated to LGBTQAI+ awareness and steps to take.

Gay YA. www.gayya.org.

> GayYA.org is a website and blog dedicated to everything LGBTQIA+ in YA literature. It encourages authors to write books with gay characters and publishers to publish them. Many book lists and other blogs are shared here.

Lo, Malinda. "My Guide to LGBT YA." *Malinda Lo* (blog), November 11, 2013. https://malinda-lo.squarespace.com/blog/2013/11/my-guide-to-lgbt-ya.

> Malinda Lo is the author of several young adult novels, most of which deal with gay and lesbian themes. This post offers an index to her LGBT-related blog entries. Great book discussions can be found here as well.

Sarles, Patricia A. *Gay-Themed Picture Books for Children.* http://booksforkidsingayfamilies.blogspot.com.

> This blog features posts about picture books for children that illustrate the experience of knowing or having a gay parent, family member, or friend as well as books for gender-nonconforming kids.

Wind, Lee. *I'm Here. I'm Queer. What the Hell Do I Read?* www.leewind.org.

> This is a blog for teens, librarians, teachers, booksellers, and other people with teens in their lives. It is for anyone interested in YA books with LGBTQAI+ characters and themes.

Glossary

lesbian: A woman who is primarily attracted (emotionally, romantically, or sexually) to other women.

gay: A person who is primarily attracted (emotionally, romantically, or sexually) to members of the same sex; can be used to refer to any sex (e.g., gay man, gay woman, gay person).

bisexual: A person who is attracted (emotionally, romantically, or sexually) to people of both their own gender and another gender; also called "bi."

transgender: A broad term commonly used to refer to people whose gender identity and/or expression is different from public expectations based on the sex they were assigned at birth. Being transgender does not signify any specific sexual orientation. Transgender people may identify as straight, gay, lesbian, bisexual, and so on.

queer: An umbrella term sometimes used by LGBTQAI+ people to refer to the entire community; often used to express fluid identities and orientations; also often used interchangeably with "LGBT."

asexual: Used to refer to a person who generally does not feel sexual attraction or desire to any group of people. Asexuality is not the same as celibacy.

intersex: Used to refer to a person whose sexual anatomy or chromosomes do not fit with the traditional features of "female" and "male"; for example, a person born with both "female" and "male" anatomy (vagina and uterus, penis and testicles).

Additional Terms

ally: A person who is not LGBTQAI+ (i.e., straight) but who shows support and promotes equality in a variety of ways.

androgynous: Used to refer to a person who identifies and/or presents as neither distinguishably masculine nor feminine.

biphobia: The expression of prejudice, fear, or hatred directed toward bisexual people.

cisgender: Used to describe a person whose gender identity aligns with that typically associated with the sex assigned at birth.

closeted: Used to describe an LGBTQAI+ person who has not disclosed his or her sexual orientation or gender identity.

coming out: The process by which a person first acknowledges, accepts, and appreciates his or her sexual orientation or gender identity and begins to share that with others.

gender dysphoria: Clinically significant distress caused when a person's assigned birth gender is not the same as the one with which he or she identifies.

gender identity: One's innermost concept of self as male, female, or a blend of both or neither—how individuals perceive themselves and what they call themselves. A person's gender identity can be the same or different from the sex assigned at birth.

gender transition: The process by which some people strive to more closely align their internal knowledge of gender with its outward appearance. Some people socially transition, whereby they might begin dressing, using names and pronouns, and/or be socially recognized as another gender. Others undergo a physical transition in which they modify their bodies through medical interventions.

gender-nonconforming: A broad term referring to people who do not behave in a way that conforms to the traditional expectations of their gender or whose gender expression does not fit neatly into a category.

genderqueer: Used to refer to people who typically reject notions of static categories of gender and who embrace fluidity of gender identity and often, though not always, sexual orientation. People who identify as genderqueer may see themselves as being both male and female, neither male nor female, or as falling completely outside these categories.

heterosexual: A person who is attracted only to members of the opposite sex; also called "straight."

homophobia: A range of negative attitudes and feelings toward homosexuality or people who are identified or perceived as being gay, lesbian, bisexual, transgender, and so on (LGBTQAI+). It can be expressed as antipathy, contempt, prejudice, aversion, or hatred; may be based on irrational fear; and is sometimes related to religious beliefs.

in the closet: Used to describe a person who keeps his or her sexual orientation or gender identity a secret from some or all people.

living openly: A state in which LGBTQAI+ people are comfortably out about their sexual orientation or gender identity—where and when it feels appropriate to them.

outing: Exposing someone's lesbian, gay, bisexual, or transgender identity to others without that person's permission. Outing someone can have serious repercussions on employment status, economic stability, personal safety, religious life, or family situations.

pansexual: A person who experiences sexual, romantic, physical, and/or spiritual attraction for members of all gender identities/expressions, not just people who fit into the standard gender binary (i.e., men and women).

questioning: Used to describe people who are in the process of exploring their sexual orientation or gender identity.

same-gender loving: A term some prefer to use instead of lesbian, gay, or bisexual to express attraction to and love for people of the same gender.

sexual orientation: An inherent or immutable, enduring emotional, romantic, or sexual attraction to other people.

transphobia: The fear and hatred of, or discomfort with, transgender people.

transsexual: A person whose gender identity is different from his or her biological sex, who may undergo medical treatments to change that biological sex, oftentimes to align it with his or her gender identity, or the person may live his or her life as another sex.

two-spirited: Used to refer to a person who has both a masculine and a feminine spirit; also used by some First Nations people to describe their sexual, gender, and/or spiritual identity. As an umbrella term, it may encompass same-sex attraction and a wide variety of gender variance, including people who might be described in Western culture as gay, lesbian, bisexual, transsexual, transgender, or genderqueer; cross-dressers; or having multiple gender identities.

Bibliography

Fewster, Peter H. "Two-Spirit Community." Researching for LGBTQ Health. Accessed July 25, 2017. http://lgbtqhealth.ca/community/two-spirit.php.

Human Rights Campaign. "Glossary of Terms." HRC.org. Accessed May 28, 2016. www.hrc.org/resources/glossary-of-terms.

Lesbian, Gay, Bisexual, Transgender, Queer, Intersex, Asexual Resource Center. "LGBTQIA Resource Center Glossary." UCDavis.edu. Accessed May 28, 2016. http://lgbtqia.ucdavis.edu/educated/glossary.html.

About the Authors

CHRISTINA DORR, PhD, teaches at Weaver Middle School, part of the Hilliard City School District, Hilliard, Ohio. She has been a media specialist for twenty-seven years and has also taught literature, literacy, technology, and library science courses for the past twelve years as an adjunct instructor for five universities in Ohio, including Kent State University and the Ohio State University, where she had earned a doctorate in education with a specialty in literature and literacy. Dorr has written book reviews and columns for various journals for many years, presented at numerous state and national organizations, and served on several book award committees for the American Library Association, including currently chairing the 2018 Stonewall Committee. This is her second coauthored book with Liz Deskins; the first was *Linking Picture Book Biographies with National Content Standards: 200+ Lives to Explore* (Libraries Unlimited 2015).

LIZ DESKINS has been a school librarian for thirty years, teaching at the elementary, high school, and college levels. She is currently teaching at Hilliard Bradley High School, in Hilliard, Ohio. She is a past president of Buckeye Children and Teens Book Awards as well as past president of OELMA (Ohio Educational Library Media Association). Liz has served on committees and task forces for the American Association of School Librarians and the Association for Library Service to Children. She also serves as Curriculum Editor for the *School Library Connection reVIEWS+* online journal, which helps to fuel her passion for writing on topics of interest to school librarians. Her latest award was the 2017 OELMA Outstanding Contributor Award, which recognizes an Ohio-licensed school librarian who has made outstanding contributions to school librarianship. A requested presenter at conferences, Liz speaks on many topics, thanks to her lifelong passion for learning new things and sharing them with others! This is her second book collaboration with Christina Dorr; the first was *Linking Picture Book Biographies to National Content Standards: 200+ Lives to Explore* (Libraries Unlimited 2015).

Subject Index

Author Index

Title Index

DATE DUE

			PRINTED IN U.S.A.